THEN AND THERE SERIES
GENERAL EDITOR
MARJORIE REEVES, M.A., Ph.D.

Wellington's Army

P F SPEED, M.A.

Illustrated from contemporary sources

LONGMAN

LONGMAN GROUP LIMITED
London

*Associated companies, branches and representatives
throughout the world*

First published 1969
Fifth impression 1978

ISBN 0 582 20455 0

Printed in Hong Kong by
The Hong Kong Printing Press Ltd

ACKNOWLEDGEMENTS

We are grateful to the following for permission to reproduce copyright material:
George Allen & Unwin Ltd for extracts from *Diary of a Cavalry Officer* by Lieutenant-
Colonel William Tomkinson; Edward Arnold (Publishers) Ltd for extracts from
Wellington's Army by Sir Charles Oman; The Clarendon Press for extracts from Vol.V
and Vol.VI of Sir Charles Oman's *History of the Peninsular War;* Peter Davies Ltd for
extracts from *The Recollections of Rifleman Harris* by Henry Curling and from *Adventures
in the Rifle Brigade* by Captain John Kincaid; Mrs. F. E. Ellis for extracts from *The
Letters of Private Wheeler* edited by Captain B. H. Liddell Hart.

The author and publisher are grateful to the following for permission to reproduce
photographs: British Museum page 47, from David Roberts' *The Military Adventures of
Johnny Newcome* 1815; The Mansell Collection pages 1 (*left*), 3 (*above and below*), 4, 5,
9, 10 (*above and below*), 12, 15 (*above*), 19, 28, 29, 33 (*above*), 35, 36, 65 and 97; the
Parker Gallery page 22 (*right*); Radio Times Hulton Picture Library pages 1 (*right*),
2, 77 and 84; W. A. Thorburn pages 100 and 101; Edward Arnold Ltd page 22 (*left*)
and 52, from Charles Oman's *Wellington's Army;* the Clarendon Press pages 21, 33
(*below*), 73 (*above*), 81 and 92, from Charles Oman's *A History of the Peninsular War;*
Heinemann Ltd pages 11 and 57 (*above and below*) from Schaumann's *On the Road with
Wellington* translated by A. Ludovic 1924; Herbert Jenkins page 24 (*above*) from Black-
more's *British Military Firearms 1650-1850* 1961; Kane and Ward Ltd page 73 (*below*),
from Jac Weller's *Wellington in the Peninsula*, taken by the author, copyright 1962
Nicholas Vane Publishers Ltd; Studio Vista page 70 from E. W. Sheppard's *A Visual
History of Modern Britain – War* 1967. We are also indebted to the Clarendon Press for
permission to base maps on those in Charles Oman's *History of the Peninsular War.*

Contents

To the Reader

Twice in this century Great Britain has had to fight a powerful enemy in Europe. Both times Germany was this enemy. More than a hundred and fifty years ago our ancestors were fighting a similar war, but their enemy was France. You will already know something about the French Revolution and Napoleon.

Britain defeated France at sea, while Germany, Austria and Russia did the most towards defeating her on land. But there was a British army as well. Although it was efficient, it was small and it could do little until it had a good general and a good opportunity.

Wellington was the general and the army found its opportunity in Spain.

This book will tell you about the ordinary soldiers of Wellington's Army and how, in many years of hard fighting, they did much more than their fair share towards overthrowing Napoleon.

Words printed in *italics* are explained in the Glossary.

1 The Outbreak of War

In 1804 Spain and France joined together under Napoleon against England. Four years later they were bitter enemies. How did this happen?

In 1804 King Charles IV of Spain and his Queen, Maria Luisa, were under the spell of a worthless minister called Godoy. Godoy slowly ruined Spain and she could do little or nothing to help Napoleon. He was not even sure that Spain would not turn against him. Napoleon decided that the King, the Queen and Godoy would have to go. Most Spaniards felt the same. They hated Godoy and would have done anything to be rid of him. But who would be their new king? The Spaniards

King Charles IV of Spain

Queen Maria Luisa

Godoy

wanted Prince Ferdinand, the heir to the throne to succeed his father, and had Napoleon supported Ferdinand, he would probably have had little trouble. But Napoleon had other plans.

In the first place he poured French troops into northern Spain, saying they were going to conquer Portugal. And the French and Spaniards did, in fact, overrun Portugal in 1807. But Napoleon sent far more men than were needed just to defeat the Portuguese. Next he invited King Charles, Queen Maria Luisa, Prince Ferdinand and Godoy to Bayonne. When they arrived he kidnapped them all and told the Spaniards that their new king was to be his own brother, Joseph Bonaparte.

The Spaniards rose in rebellion against Napoleon, and each province elected its own *junta*. Under Godoy's misrule the Spanish army had become almost useless, so the juntas raised what forces they could and made ready to meet Napoleon's veterans. Of course, the well-organised French armies usually defeated the Spaniards, but they did not have it all their own way. One French army marched too far to the south. The Spaniards surrounded them and made them surrender.

Street fighting in Madrid

Fight between French soldiers and Spanish civilians

The Maid of Saragossa

A young girl, Agostina Zaragoza, showed the spirit of Spain. The French were attacking Saragossa; they had broken through the walls and it seemed as if the town must fall. Agostina's lover had loaded his cannon and was about to fire when he was shot dead. The French saw this and came on. The Spanish troops turned to run, but Agostina jumped forward. She picked up the burning *match* and fired the gun. Blasted with *grape shot* at point blank range, the French fell back. The Spaniards turned again to take up the fight and the town was saved.

What did the British think about the war? By 1808 they were fighting Napoleon with all their strength and were determined to defeat him. Since Nelson's victory at Trafalgar in 1805, the French had not been a danger at sea. But Napoleon's armies were still winning victories in Europe. Our own army had been able to do little. But now, at last, Napoleon had given us an opportunity. He had made enemies of Spain and Portugal, and Spain seemed determined to resist him to the last. The British government decided to help. They sent ship loads of weapons

Troops and guns landing

and supplies for the Spaniards, and on 1 August 1808 a British army of 13,000 landed in Portugal. There were British soldiers in the *Iberian Peninsula* from then until 1814.

What kind of country were our troops fighting in, and what did they think of its inhabitants?

2 The Iberian Peninsula and its Inhabitants

The Iberian Peninsula is Spain and Portugal together. Its total area is 230,000 square miles, or about four times as big as England and Wales. Wellington's men had to march long distances.

Much of the country is difficult. There are large rolling plains, ideal for cavalry, but there are mountain ranges as well. You should look at the map at the end of the book and find some of these mountains. At the same time you can find the rivers and learn the names of some of them.

Rivers can often help armies. Soldiers can carry supplies up them in barges and often they can use them to hold up an enemy. But the rivers of Spain and Portugal are not like that. In many places they flow much too swiftly for barges, nor are they good barriers. In summer they dry up so much that it is often easy to ford them. No general could feel safe because he had put a river between himself and his enemy.

The climate is as difficult as the country. All through the summer it is dry and very hot. Troops often had to march long distances in great heat before they could find water. But in autumn and winter there could be heavy rains that soaked men to the skin and turned the road surfaces into a deep sticky mud that would drag the boots off a man's feet.

There are also big differences in temperature. Near Lisbon our soldiers found they could bathe in the rivers all through the winter. But high in the mountains, away from the sea, the winters are biting. Men who had become used to the south coast suffered if they had suddenly to go inland.

Country and climate were unfriendly. But what about the

inhabitants? The British had mixed feelings about both the Portuguese and the Spaniards.

The Portuguese
The English found that the Portuguese were poor and dirty. An English private wrote:

'What an ignorant, superstitious, priest-ridden, dirty, lousy set of poor Devils are the Portuguese.' The streets he says were full of 'half starved dogs, fat Priests and lousy people'. 'In the middle of the day the sunny sides of the streets swarm with men and women picking vermin from their bodies, and it is no uncommon sight to see two respectably dressed persons meet and do a friendly office for each other by picking a few crawlers from each other's persons.'

A doctor with the army described the life of a parish priest. He said the priest lived with his mother in a two roomed hovel. 'They had no servants and the domestic duties appeared to be performed by the poor old woman. She was without shoes and the earthen muddy floor was in different places imprinted with the shape of her large feet. He told me that in winter he and his mother lived entirely on bacon and chestnuts, and showed me where these were piled up in the corner.'

Because they were so poor the Portuguese were not able to pay much money towards the cost of the war. But they could find men. In 1809 the Portuguese government made an English officer, General Beresford, commander-in-chief of their army. Beresford found the army in a bad state. There were many old and useless officers, but only 30,000 troops where there should have been 60,000. Beresford sacked the useless officers, made the regiments up to strength and brought large numbers of English officers into the Portuguese army. Weapons and equipment came from England, and the new officers drilled and disciplined the men until they were good soldiers. We shall see later how Wellington fitted the Portuguese regiments into his own army. Without them he could have done very little. For example, at the Battle of Salamanca he had 30,000 British troops and the French had 50,000. He was able to fight a battle, because along with his British troops were 18,000 Portuguese.

The Spaniards

The Spaniards of Wellington's day must have been the most exasperating allies this country has had. The problem of working with them came out in 1809 when Wellington tried to co-operate with General Cuesta, the Captain General of Estremadura.

The very sight of Cuesta was bad enough. His cavalry had fled in panic a few days before and had ridden over him. As a result he could only stay on a horse if two men held him there. Wellington reviewed the Spanish army and was even more horrified. Many of the regiments were without boots or proper weapons.

The next discovery was also unpleasant. The Spaniards had promised to send food to the English, but all Wellington had from them was promises.

However the English and Spaniards did have a stroke of luck and caught the French army under General Victor unawares. Wellington rode over to Cuesta and urged him to attack. He found the Spaniard having a nap. When he woke up all he would say was that he would not fight a battle on a Sunday— and that was that. The next day, after he had lost his chance, Cuesta was anxious to attack. He dashed after Victor with his entire army. Wellington refused to move. He knew that Victor was going to join King Joseph, who had powerful reinforcements. He let Cuesta go and settled down to wait. Sure enough in a few days' time, back came the Spaniards in a panic. The French were coming.

Cuesta now camped his army in a position he could never defend, and with his back to a river, so that his men could not escape. Wellington begged the stubborn old man to draw his army back a mile or so and take up an excellent position beside the English. Cuesta said he would not retreat another step. Wellington pleaded with him. Cuesta still refused. At last Wellington fell on his knees and begged the Spaniard to join him. At this the old man's Spanish pride was satisfied, and he moved his army into line with Wellington's, near the town of Talavera.

In the battle that followed the French were defeated, but

almost all the fighting was done by the British. The Spaniards could not *manoeuvre*, so they stayed in position and the French ignored them. There was an extraordinary incident right at the beginning of the battle. A few French cavalry rode in front of the Spaniards. They were too few to matter and were, in any case, out of range. But every man in the Spanish army fired his musket. This enormous *volley* did no harm to the enemy, but five Spanish battalions were so scared by the noise of their own muskets that they fled. An English officer turned to Wellington and gasped, 'Did you see that my lord?' 'Yes,' said Wellington, 'and damn me if I ever saw ten thousand men run a race before.'

Talavera taught Wellington his lesson. Never again did he try to work closely with a Spanish force unless he was sure that their commander would co-operate. He did find helpful Spanish generals, but for the most part he let the Spaniards go their own way.

But none the less, the Spaniards did a lot towards winning the war. The more the French ill-treated them, the more stubborn they became. One French commander called Abbé said he would go on taking hostages and shooting them until the Spaniards in his province gave up resistance. The local *guerrilla* captain said that for every Spaniard shot, he would take and kill four Frenchmen. This he did until Abbé withdrew his vicious order.

An Execution

Above: *shooting a hostage*   Below: *soldiers attacking civilians*

The Spanish regular army was pathetic, but its generals kept on fighting pitched battles with the French. Time and again they were defeated and the men scattered. Yet one by one they rejoined their units only to go on to yet another defeat. But all through the war there were Spanish armies in the field, and as soon as the French left a province, they moved into it.

Even more effective than the field army were the guerrilla bands. An English officer said of them:

'They are complete *banditti*, two-thirds clothed in things taken from the enemy. The only pay they receive is from plunder. The country provides them with regular rations.

'They are of no use when before the enemy, but are excellent in gaining information and surprising small detachments. At the time the enemy occupied Medino del Campo before our advance, they could not send out a single *wood party* under two hundred men and one night the Guerrillas took 40 horses and two *dragoons* out of the square of the town.'

Because of the guerrillas, many French troops had to do garrison duty and patrol the main roads. Despatch riders could not travel in some parts of Spain unless they had an escort of hundreds of soldiers. Indeed in 1813 the guerrillas cut King Joseph's communications with France, and he had neither supplies nor letters for weeks.

With an Anglo-Portuguese army of only 60,000 Wellington was able to make war against the French who had at one time 300,000 men in the Peninsula. This was because of the Spaniards. The French knew that if they drew in their scattered forces the Spaniards would at once rise in rebellion behind them.

3   The Duke of Wellington

When he was christened Wellington's name was Arthur Wesley. Later he changed it to Arthur Wellesley. He took the title of Wellington when he was made a Viscount after his victory at Talavera in 1809. He became Duke in 1814. It will save confusion if we call him 'Wellington' all the time.

When he took command of the British army in the Peninsula in 1809 he was thirty-nine years old. You can see a picture of him below. He was of average height, and was lean and wiry. His eyes were cold and grey, but the most striking thing about his face was his nose. One day a drunken private called out that he was 'the long-nosed beggar that licks the French'. Most of the troops called him 'Nosey'.

Wellington

Some great generals have been popular. Napoleon was. He used to joke with his men, pull their noses and march alongside them. Wellington was just the opposite. Once he said of his men: 'They are the scum of the earth. English soldiers are fellows who have enlisted for drink—that is the plain fact; they have ALL enlisted for drink.'

He was very good at biting retorts. In later years a gentleman asked him if he had not been surprised at Waterloo. 'No,' said Wellington, 'but I am now.' Once during the war in Spain he ordered General Craufurd to bring his troops back to join the main army immediately. This would have meant a night march and Craufurd decided to wait until morning. As a result he arrived half a day late. Wellington greeted Craufurd with, 'I am glad to see you safe.' 'Oh, I was in no danger, I assure you,' said Craufurd . 'No,' said Wellington, 'but I was, from your conduct.' Craufurd stumped off muttering, 'He's damned crusty today.'

But if the men in his army had little liking for Wellington, they had every confidence in him. One officer wrote:

'As a general action seemed now to be inevitable, we anxiously longed for the return of Lord Wellington, as we would rather see his long nose in the fight than a reinforcement of ten thousand men any day. I'll venture to say that there was not a heart in that army that did not beat more lightly when we heard the joyful news of his arrival, the day before the enemy's advance.'

Wellington cared for the lives of his troops. The men knew this and respected him for it. It was far better to be commanded by the cold, haughty Wellington, than by the friendly, jovial Napoleon, who boasted that the lives of a million men were of no importance to him.

Wellington had great courage, and had taught himself to be calm in all sorts of dangers. On the way out to Portugal the ship ran into a storm. As Wellington was undressing for the night, a servant came running into his cabin, shouting that all was lost. 'In that case,' came the reply, 'I shall not bother to take off my boots.'

4   The Officers

In Wellington's day the usual way to become an officer was to buy a *commission*. A wealthy father might buy his son of fifteen or sixteen an *ensign's* commission. As senior officers retired or moved on, their positions went up for sale, and provided he had the money, a young man could buy himself quick promotion.

What happened to a man who had no money? The outlook for him was not at all bright, however good he might be. It was just possible to become an ensign without purchase, but it would not be in a good regiment. After that you could only win promotion if the officer immediately above you was killed in battle.

One unfortunate officer was Lieutenant Dyas. He led a desperate attack on Badajoz in 1811. When he came back his cap had been hit off, his sword shot off close to the hilt, his *scabbard* was gone, and the laps of his coat were full of bullet holes. In spite of all this he insisted on leading a second attack the following day. Years later this brave man was still only a lieutenant.

It was very unusual for a private soldier to become an officer. There were a few men promoted from the ranks, but most of them were not good officers. The men disliked them. They knew too many of the old soldier's tricks to be popular.

A few officers were tyrannical bullies who broke the spirits of their men; more were careless and inefficient. One day when Wellington had read a list of some officers who were going to join him he said, 'I only hope that when the enemy reads this list, he trembles as much as I do.'

But strange though it may seem, the system of purchase produced far more good officers than bad ones. Wellington, who knew all the snags, defended it to the end of his days.

One of Wellington's
Generals—Sir Thomas Picton

Purchase, he said, was the only way to make sure the army was officered by gentlemen.

A cavalry officer that you will read about in this book was Lieutenant William Tomkinson of the 16th Light Dragoons. He first came to the Peninsula in 1809, but was wounded soon after he arrived. He went back home to recover, and returned about a year later. He then stayed in Spain until 1813. He was at the Battle of Waterloo and escaped unhurt. After the war he rose to the rank of Lieutenant-Colonel. Here is a picture of him.

William Tomkinson

The light cavalry spent a lot of time scouting and keeping watch on the enemy, so William Tomkinson had an exciting time.

I do not think Tomkinson can have been very popular. He kept a diary which we can still read. In it he often makes unkind remarks about his fellow officers. He only seems to have made one close friend, Major Charles Somers Cocks. Cocks was killed at the siege of Burgos in 1812, and Tomkinson was broken-hearted.

A quite different man was Captain John Kincaid. He was with the famous 95th Regiment. This was a Light Infantry unit, armed with *rifles*. Riflemen thought themelves rather special, and John Kincaid said: 'We were the light regiment of the Light Division and fired the first and last shot in almost every battle, siege and skirmish, in which the army was engaged during the war.' Like Tomkinson, Kincaid kept a diary. He filled his pages with lively, colourful stories that tell us a lot about the daily life of Wellington's men.

Rank
Army ranks were much the same in Wellington's day as they are now, so you could look them up for yourself in a Reference Library. The only difference was that the lowest ranking officer was called an 'ensign.' What is he called today?

5 The Men

All Wellington's men were volunteers. Some of them joined the army straight from civilian life; others came from the *militia*. The militia was there to defend the country against invasion, and militiamen could not be sent overseas. Men were forced to join. There was a ballot from time to time to pick the unlucky ones. It was unpleasant in the militia, but there was only one way to escape from it, and that was to join the regular army. But if you did that you could be sent to fight overseas, and you would be lucky to come home alive. Why, then, did men join the army? Some were in trouble—they were in debt, they had committed a crime, they had fallen out with their wives or parents. Others liked what they imagined was the glamour of the army, and still more wanted the *bounty money*, for each man who joined had anything from £10 to £25. Sometimes officers commanding the militia made life unpleasant for their men in order to drive them into the army. You can judge for yourself by reading these stories about recruiting. One man wrote:

'The militia would be drawn up in line, and the officers of the regiments requiring volunteers would give a glowing description of their several corps, describing the victories they had gained, and the honours they had acquired, and conclude by offering the bounty. If these inducements were not effectual in getting men, *coercive measures* were adopted; the militia colonel would put on heavy and long drills and field exercises, which were so tedious and oppressive that many men would embrace the alternative and volunteer for the *regulars*.'

A man called Harris says why he joined the famous 95th regiment: 'I one day saw a corps of the 95th Rifles and so fell in love with their smart, dashing and devil-may-care appearance

that nothing would serve me till I was a rifleman myself.'
Later Harris himself went recruiting, along with the serjeant-major of the 95th. Their first recruit was a sweep they met in a public house. He said to them:

' "There's nothing against my being a soldier but my black face; I'm strong, active and healthy and able to lick the best man in this room."

' "Hang your black face," said the serjeant-major; "The rifles can't be too dark; you're a strong rascal, and if you mean it, we'll take you to the doctor tomorrow, and make a general of you the next day." So we had the sweep that night into a large tub of water, scoured him outside and filled him with punch inside and made a Rifleman of him.'

Later Harris and the serjeant-major went to see some militiamen:

'When on recruiting service in those days, men were accustomed to make as gallant a show as they could, and accordingly we smartened up a trifle. The serjeant-major was quite a *beau* in his way; he had a sling belt to his sword like a field officer, a tremendous green feather in his cap, a flaring sash, his whistle and powder flask displayed, an officer's *pelisse* over one shoulder, and a double allowance of ribbons in his cap; whilst I myself was as smart as I dared appear, with my rifle slung at my shoulder.

'We worked hard at this business; I may say that for three days and nights we kept up the dance and drunken riot. Every volunteer got ten guineas bounty, which, except for two kept back for necessaries, they spent in every sort of excess, till all was gone. Then came the reaction. The drooping spirits, the grief at parting with old comrades, sweethearts and wives, for the uncertain fate of war. And then came the jeers of the old soldier; the laughter of myself and comrades, and our attempts to give a *fillip* to their spirits as we marched them off from the friends they were never to look upon again.'

There were bad recruits. These were the men who would later plunder and ill-treat peasants, rob and attack their comrades, and desert to the enemy. Others who were not actually criminals were rowdy and unruly. The ruffians won the army a bad name, but they were only a minority. There were others who were religious almost to a fault. Some took to preaching. One man was ashamed of the way he sometimes lost his temper and hit people. His landlord annoyed him and he knocked him down. He decided this should be the last time, and, remembering the text, 'If thy right hand offend thee, cut it off', he took an axe, placed his hand on a windowsill and lopped it off.

Most of the soldiers were neither saints nor criminals. They were ordinary fellows, perhaps rougher than average, but not bad at heart.

Not many of Wellington's ordinary soldiers kept diaries, but we do have an excellent collection of letters that Private William Wheeler wrote home to his family in Bath. They are full of exciting stories. Probably Wheeler was not a typical private. He had some education, and was very well behaved. He was never drunk and never in trouble. By the end of the war he had been promoted to serjeant.

Wheeler came to Spain in 1809. He was wounded in 1813 and was a long time recovering. However, he was at the battle of Waterloo and, luckily, he escaped from this unhurt.

Foreigners in the Army
The most important group of foreigners were the Portuguese, and you have already found out something about these. But there were also Germans and even Frenchmen.

King George III of England was also the ruler of Hanover in North-West Germany. When the French captured Hanover, many men escaped to England to go on with the fight. These Germans called themselves the King's German Legion. Wellington had with him four of their cavalry regiments and five of their infantry battalions. They were very good soldiers.

The French with Wellington called themselves the 'Chasseurs Britanniques'. Most of their officers were royalists who hated Napoleon more than the British did. But too many of the ordinary soldiers were unreliable. A lot of them were prisoners of war who pretended they wanted to join our army; in fact all they wanted was a chance to escape back to their own side.

6 The Infantry

Organisation

If you had asked one of Wellington's men which was his unit, he would have told you his regiment. The regiment was like his family. Most men, particularly officers, were very proud of their regiment. They would fight a duel with anyone who insulted it. They looked on the colours as almost sacred.

But no regiment even went to war as a body. No one would ever describe an army as being so many regiments strong, since regiments could be different sizes, and since each one would have a large number of men in England. The unit that counted on the battlefield was the battalion. Most regiments had two battalions. One, usually the first battalion, would be on active service abroad, and the other, the second battalion, would be at home, at the regimental *depôt*. The first battalion would keep up its numbers by taking men from the second battalion. The second battalion would then take in recruits and drill and train them until they, too, went overseas.

There were, however, quite a number of single battalion regiments. They made up their depôt by leaving about a fifth of their men at home. They could never put as many men in the field as two battalion regiments. There were a few regiments with three battalions, and one that had five, but it was unusual to have more than two.

At full strength a first battalion had 1,000 privates and about 100 other ranks, made up of officers, N.C.O.s and musicians. If the regiment had but one battalion, then it would only have 800 men in the field at full strength. But a battalion was rarely at full strength. Even for the larger battalions 700 or 800 would be a normal size, and it could work down to about 400.

Each battalion was divided into ten companies, which as you will realise should be 80 or 100 strong.

Battalions did not usually work alone. Normally they were in threes, and this group was called a brigade. When Wellington arrived in the Peninsula the brigade was the largest unit in the army. He found that this would not do, as he could not handle an army consisting of so many small pieces. The brigades would have to be grouped in divisions.

Portuguese Infantryman

It needed a lot of thought how best to make up a division, as Portuguese troops had to be included in the army. Finally Wellington decided that most of his divisions should have two British brigades and one Portuguese. A Portuguese brigade consisted of five battalions, and was nearly as big as the two English brigades put together.

At first there were five divisions in the army. Later there were seven. In addition, there was the famous Light Division. This was much smaller than the others, for it had only three British battalions and two Portuguese. But, as we shall see, it had special training, special weapons, and special duties.

Uniform

Below left you can see a picture of an ordinary soldier. His hat was called a 'shako'. It had a brass plate in front with the number of his regiment, a woollen tuft on one side in the regimental colours, a peak and a chin-strap. You will see that it is narrower at the crown than it is at the base. The French shako

Private Soldier

French Soldier

was the opposite, so it was usually easy to tell friend from foe. Shakos were made of felt, and they soon lost their colour and their shape. One soldier wrote: 'Distorted by alternate rain and sunshine as well as by having served as pillows and nightcaps, our caps had assumed the most monstrous and grotesque shapes.'

The coat was cut short in the front, but had tails at the back. Its colour was red. You will have heard of the 'redcoats' and 'the thin red line'. For ornament there were white stripes running across from the buttons. There were two white cross belts. One of these held the man's bayonet, and the other his *cartouche box*. The infantryman wore trousers, and these were a big improvement on the old breeches and gaiters which had taken ten minutes to put on. In fact the only inconvenient thing about this uniform was the high collar, stiffened with leather stocks.

The troops were also lucky because Wellington did not bother men about their uniforms. An officer wrote: 'Provided we brought our men into the field well appointed, with their sixty rounds of ammunition each, he never looked to see whether trousers were black, blue or grey; and as to ourselves we might be clad in any colour of the rainbow if we fancied it.'

Towards the end of the war one regiment caused a sensation by marching into a French town wearing trousers made from blankets.

The private soldier carried all his kit himself in a *knapsack* of oilskin or glazed canvas. Private Wheeler says he carried a blanket, a greatcoat, two shirts, two pairs of stockings, two pairs of boots, one pair of soles and heels, a *canteen* of water, rations for three days and sixty rounds of ammunition. 'All this', he complained, 'was load enough for a donkey.' It weighed about sixty pounds—well over half a hundredweight.

Weapons

The infantryman fought with a musket. The correct name for it was the 'Tower musket' but the soldiers called it 'Brown Bess'. It weighed about nine pounds.

Before going into action each soldier was supposed to make up

23

Musket

sixty paper cartridges. Each cartridge would be a tube containing the right amount of gunpowder and a round lead bullet. It had to be rammed down the barrel with a rod. In the picture

Soldier using ramrod

on page 24 you can see where this rod was stored. Raw recruits sometimes forgot to take the rod out of the barrel, shot it away and were left helpless. Having rammed home the cartridge, the soldier had to place a little loose powder in his pan. You can see this pan in the diagram below. He cocked the musket by pulling back the hammer holding the flint. When he pulled the trigger, the hammer fell down, and the flint struck on the steel. This did two things. It shot up the lid of the pan, and it showered sparks on the loose powder inside it. This then caught fire and sent a flame through the touch hole. This in turn set off the main charge. Below you can also see the lock of a musket before and after firing.

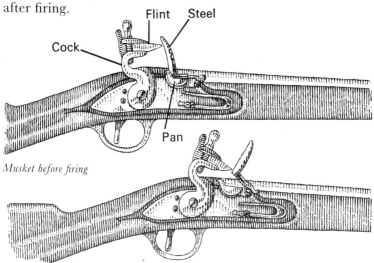

Musket before firing

Musket after firing

Muskets did not always go off. You can imagine how difficult it was to use them in the rain. The cartouche box might leak; the cartridge the man was handling might easily become wet; nothing would be easier than for damp to find its way into the pan.

If all was well, the Brown Bess would fire a ball three hundred yards. However, it was almost impossible to be sure of hitting anything more than a hundred yards away.

Wellington's men could fire their muskets every fifteen seconds, which was remarkably fast.

Light Infantry

So far we have been talking about soldiers of the 'line'. But there were many troops who were not in the line. These were the 'light infantry'. They had this name because they had to march and manoeuvre quickly and easily. Sir John Moore had been very interested in these troops and had formed a training school for them at Shorncliffe. Light infantry were of various kinds.

In the first place there were the riflemen. A rifle has corkscrew-like grooves cut in its barrel. These make the bullet spin as it flies forward, and a bullet that spins is more accurate than one that does not. The disadvantage with the rifle was that it took longer to load than the musket—it was more difficult to force the bullet down the barrel because of the grooves.

The rifleman wore a dark green uniform, because he often needed to take cover and a red coat makes a man easy to see. You can see a picture of a rifleman and an officer of rifles below.

A rifleman   *An officer of rifles*

Many of the riflemen of Wellington's army were in the famous Rifle Brigade, which formed part of the Light Division.

Apart from the rifle battalions there were various regiments who had the same training, but who were armed with a special light-weight musket. Also in each battalion the smaller and more lively men were put in a light company of their own.

Finally there were the Portuguese *caçadores,* or riflemen. Each Portuguese brigade was made up of five battalions, and one of these was a rifle battalion.

You will see how Wellington used his light infantry later on in this chapter.

Infantry Tactics
In the eighteenth century generals had usually drawn up their infantry in three ranks, with cavalry on either wing. Rival armies closed on each other in this formation and fought it out. The cavalry charged one another and the infantry fired volleys. You won the battle if your cavalry could chase away the enemy's and fall on the flank of his infantry, or if your infantry were the better musketeers. These troops were highly trained professional soldiers, and it needed good training as well as courage to stand firm in a line only three ranks deep.

But after the Revolution, French armies were made up of half-disciplined recruits. The only advantage they had was in numbers. How could the French use their numbers to advantage against the steady, well-drilled troops of countries like Austria and Prussia?

First of all they took the best men and trained them as *tirailleurs,* or skirmishers. These men did not have to keep any set formation. Instead they advanced like a swarm of angry bees. Whenever they found a bit of cover—a bush, a tree, a rock, or a dip in the ground—they would stop and take pot shots at the enemy line. If the enemy line advanced, they would beat a hasty retreat. If the line stayed still, they would kill and wound the men in it or draw their fire.

Protected by this crowd of tirailleurs, the rest of the infantry advanced in solid blocks, called columns. There would be several columns advancing at various points. When they drew

French cavalry charge

near the enemy the cloud of skirmishers would give way and the columns would rush at the enemy, cheering and shouting. If the skirmishers had done their work, the soldiers of the line would already be badly shaken and at the onslaught of the solid masses of the columns they would break and run.

Later, the French armies improved and Napoleon made these tactics even more deadly by the use of artillery and cavalry. Now the soldiers of the line had more than the tirailleurs to face. Round shot came bounding along the ground, shells blasted holes in their ranks, and then, out of the clouds of smoke would come a mass of galloping horsemen, or the wildly cheering columns.

What were the British to do in the face of these new tactics? In the first place they realised how valuable the swarm of skirmishers could be, and they determined to have their own. These were the light infantry you read about earlier on. The men were taught to act and think for themselves, to shoot straight, to hold up the enemy for as long as possible, but to fall back fighting the whole way if hard pressed. 'Fire and retire' was one of their best-known bugle calls.

French cavalry officer

The light infantry, then, would take care of the tirailleurs. But how was it possible to stop the columns? The British took a bold decision. They reduced their line from three ranks to two. This might seem foolish, but it was not. When troops were in three ranks, only the first two could fire, but when they were in two ranks, every man could use his musket. Supposing a French battalion, about 600 strong, advanced in a column of double companies—that is sixty-six ranks wide and nine ranks deep—only the front two ranks, or 132 men, could fire. On the other hand, the men of an English battalion of the same size could use all their six hundred muskets. By simple arithmetic, the column must be defeated, if only the troops in the line stood firm. British troops did.

Wellington thought long and hard about these problems. He, too, was sure that the line could defeat the column, but only

29

under the proper conditions. He thought three things were essential.

1. The line must have its *flanks* protected. If enemy cavalry could catch the line from the side, then they would roll it up. But there were many ways of giving protection to the flanks. Obviously a *ravine* would keep off cavalry, so would a village or wood full of skirmishers. If there was nothing on the field of battle to help, then the army could provide its own protection, with a square of infantry or a body of cavalry.

2. The line must be protected in front, by skirmishers. Wellington increased his light troops even more. In each division of about 5,000 men over 1,200 were skirmishers. These were more than enough to keep off the French tirailleurs. In fact the latter very rarely got anywhere near the British line, and were so hard pressed that they could not protect their own columns. It was the turn of the column to be peppered, harassed and disorganised by skilful sharpshooters who swarmed all round it.

3. The last of Wellington's principles was that the line was not to show itself to the enemy until the last minute. His favourite position was on top of a hill—not on the crest where his enemy could pound him with gunfire, but drawn back a distance. Only when the column was within range would the men in the line stand up to fire.

This is what a Frenchman said about an attack on an English line:

'When we got to about one thousand yards from the English line, our men would begin to get restless and excited; they exchanged ideas with one another, their march began to be somewhat *precipitate*, and was already growing a little disorderly. Meanwhile the English, silent and impassive with grounded arms loomed like a long red wall; their aspect was imposing. Soon the distance began to grow shorter; cries of 'Vive l'Empereur' broke from our mass. Some men hoisted their shakos on their muskets, the quick-step became a run; the ranks began to be mixed up; the men's agitation became tumultuous, many soldiers began to fire as they ran. And all the while the red English line, still silent and motionless, even when we were only three hundred yards away, seemed to take no notice of the storm that was about to beat upon it.

The contrast was striking. More than one of us began to reflect that the enemy's fire, so long reserved, would be very unpleasant when it did break forth. Our ardour began to cool.

At this moment of painful expectation the English line would make a quarter turn—the muskets were going up to the 'ready'. An indefinable sensation nailed to the spot many of our men, who halted and opened a wavering fire. The enemy's return, a volley of simultaneous precision and deadly effect, crashed in upon us like a thunderbolt. Decimated by it we reeled together, staggering under the blow and trying to recover our equilibrium. Then three formidable 'Hurrahs' terminated the long silence of our adversaries. With the third they were down upon us with the bayonet, pressing us into a disorderly retreat. But to our great surprise they did not pursue their advantage for more than some hundred yards and went back with calm to their former lines to wait for another attack. We rarely failed to deliver it when our reinforcements came up—with the same want of success, and heavier losses.'

7 The Cavalry

Organisation

There were cavalry regiments, just as there were infantry regiments. At full strength each had just over 900 men. But no cavalry regiment had more than one battalion, so, like single battalion infantry regiments, they had to leave men at home to make up a depôt. Because of this, and because of sickness among men and horses, a regiment in the field was lucky if it was 450 strong.

In each regiment there were three or four squadrons, and in each squadron, there were ten troops. Two or three regiments made up a brigade, but there were no cavalry divisions.

Weapons

Cavalrymen carried pistols, and sometimes light muskets called carbines. But they used their *sabres* more than their firearms. A sabre was a sword with a slight curve. A cavalryman did not thrust with it, like a fencer, but slashed in the same way you would cut down nettles with a stick. A good blow with the sabre would take off a man's head.

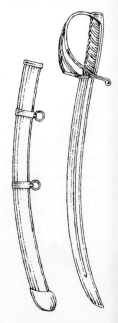

Cavalry sabre and scabbard

Cavalry fight

But the most important weapon a cavalryman had was his horse. If you have ever stood near a galloping horse, you will have some idea of what it was like to face a cavalry charge.

Tactics

Wellington depended mainly on his infantry. There were several reasons for this. In the first place he had very few cavalry. In 1809 he had only eight British regiments, and by 1810 only six. Nor could he make up numbers with Portuguese, for Portugal was short of horses. At the Battle of Salamanca there were only 500 Portuguese cavalry. Secondly, much of the fighting down to 1812 took place in Portugal which is rugged and mountainous, and quite unsuitable for cavalry.

Portuguese dragoon

33

During 1812 the number of cavalry regiments went up to sixteen and the war moved into the plains of central Spain. But still Wellington did not use his cavalry to the full. He did not trust them. After the war he wrote: 'I considered our cavalry so inferior to the French from want of order, that although I considered one of our squadrons a match for two French, yet I did not care to see four British opposed to four French, and still more so as the numbers increased and order became more necessary. They could gallop, but could not preserve their order.'

Major General Slade proved this point. In June 1812 he had with him two splendid regiments, the 1st Royals and the 3rd Dragoon Guards—six squadrons in all. He met the French general L'Allemand who also had six squadrons. While Slade charged with all his men, L'Allemand put one of his squadrons in reserve, and hid it out of sight. Slade's men defeated the five squadrons in front of them, but then got so excited that they broke up and chased the French in a disorderly mob. All went well enough until they drew level with L'Allemand's reserve squadron. This charged them in flank and rear while the men who had been running away turned and fought. Had Slade kept his men in order, he could have fought back, but they were so scattered that no one could do anything. The British fled, and the French killed many of them. Wellington was disgusted. He wrote: 'I have never been more annoyed than by Slade's affair. Our officers of cavalry have acquired the trick of galloping at everything. They never consider the situation, never think of manoeuvring before an enemy, and never keep back or provide for a reserve.'

As we shall see one brigade behaved well at the Battle of Salamanca, but this was about the only time in the war that British cavalry did anything important in a great battle.

What, then, did Wellington do with his cavalry? In the first place he used it for reconnaissance. Small parties would ride round the French armies and send back information. Secondly, he used cavalry as a screen, to keep the enemy from the main army while it was in camp, or on the march. When on this job the cavalry usually worked with the Light Division, and you

Cavalry

can read what it was like in the sections on Advance Guard and Rear Guard in Chapter 11.

Cavalry against Infantry

Quite often English and French cavalry would meet, and there were many exciting little battles. Sometimes one side won, and sometimes the other. But when cavalry met infantry the result was nearly always a stale-mate. The infantry would throw themselves into a square, with each side three ranks deep. The front rank knelt and the two others stood. In this way they formed a hedge of bayonets that no horse would charge. Troops could even march in a square and keep off cavalry. At one battle in 1811 the Light Division, in five squares, fell back two miles, surrounded by enemy cavalry the whole way. Kintaid said with pride: 'The execution of our movement presented a magnificent military spectacle, as the plain was by this time in the possession of the French cavalry, and, while we were retiring through it with the order and precision of a common field day, they kept dancing around us, and every instant threatening a charge without daring to execute it.'

Cavalry attack a square

No properly formed British square ever broke during the war, and the French infantry did nearly as well.

But if infantry on their own tried to fight a mixed force, it was a different story. If the enemy had some guns with them, they could first of all shoot the squares to pieces before sending in the cavalry. And infantry met cavalry and infantry at Salamanca, with spectacular results, as you will see.

8   The Artillery

All the guns in Wellington's day worked in the same way. The only difference was in size. Here is a picture of a gun:

Gun and limber

This gun is 'limbered up.' The carriage is hooked on to the *limber* and the gun is ready to be pulled away. The picture on pages 38-39 shows a gun crew moving their gun. Now here is a gun 'unlimbered,' and ready for firing:

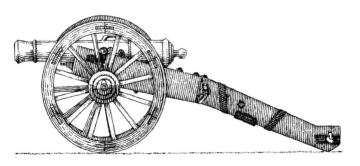

Gun unlimbered

Gun on the move

This diagram shows you how to load a gun:

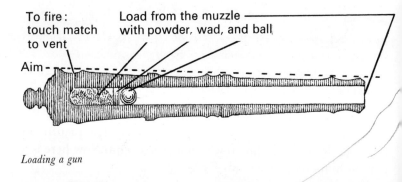

To fire:
touch match
to vent

Load from the muzzle ——————
with powder, wad, and ball

Aim -

Loading a gun

To push the charge home the gunner used a rammer. After he had fired his gun he wiped it out with a damp sponge. There might be sparks left behind and it was important to put these out before placing more powder in the gun! Here are pictures of a rammer and a sponge:

In the early days of cannon, gunners had poured the gunpowder into their guns using a marked ladle in much the same way that your mother uses a measuring jug; in Wellington's day they used 'fixed ammunition'. You can see that instead of the wad there is a 'sabot'. Sabots were made of paper or compressed wood chips. First of all the cannon ball, or 'shot' is strapped to the sabot and then a powder bag is tied below. This meant you could load the gun all in one go, which was much quicker. Here you see a picture of 'fixed Ammunition'.

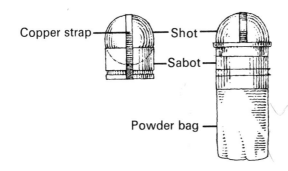

Copper strap — — Shot
— Sabot

Powder bag —

There were different kinds of shot:

1. *Round shot.* This was just a round ball of iron. Round shot was the thing for breaking down the walls of a fortress. It could also be used against the enemy guns in a fortress. You tried to

39

lob your shot just over the *parapet,* when it would bounce along like a marble on a stone floor and, if you were lucky, do a lot of damage.

Round shot could also do a lot of harm to soldiers in the field. Men fought side by side and were good targets. If you could send a round shot bouncing in among them, you could kill a large number. It was lucky for the British that it rained heavily the night before the battle of Waterloo. The French shot sank into the soft ground at the spot where it landed.

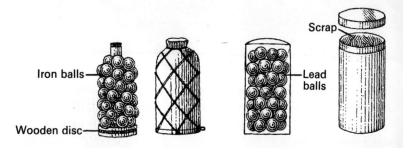

Grape shot and case shot

2. *Grape shot and case, or canister.* The diagrams show you how this was made up. In grape shot the iron balls were arranged round a core and then held in place with a canvas bag and a net. Can you see why grape shot was so called? In case shot the balls or scrap were put in a light metal box that just fitted the barrel of the gun.

Firing grape or case was rather like flinging a handful of loose stones.

3. *Bombs or shells.* These were round, but hollow. Sometimes they held only gunpowder, and it was the case of the shell bursting to pieces that did the damage. Sometimes they held a mixture of gunpowder and iron balls. You can see there is a fuse running down the middle. It was the blast from the gun that lit this. The fuse would explode the bursting charge just as the shell landed among the enemy, or even in the air above them.

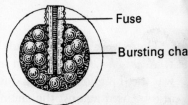

Shells were horrible. It was frightening if one fell near you. The fuse would be fizzing away, and there would be no telling when it would go off—but there would almost certainly not be enough time to escape. An English officer describes what happened when one shell landed: 'I saw one shell drop in the middle of a Portuguese regiment in close column immediately in our rear; it blew up twelve men who became so scorched and blackened that on their fall they resembled a group of mutilated chimney sweeps.'

Guns came in different sizes. They were classed according to the weight of shot they could fire. There were enormous siege guns that would throw a cannon ball of 48 pounds—but Wellington had none of these with him. It would have been impossible to move them along the roads of the Peninsula. His siege guns were 24 pounders, and even these were difficult to move. An army that wanted to move quickly could not take siege guns with it. Guns used in battle, against troops, were called field guns. The smaller field guns were 4 or 6 pounders, and it was easy enough to move them. The picture on page 38 shows a light field gun. This is horse artillery. It had this name because the men of the crew all rode on horseback, or on the limber. The heavier field guns moved so slowly that their crews could keep up with them on foot.

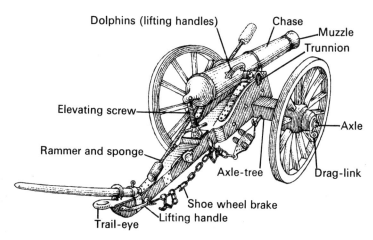

Parts of a gun

9 Supplies

The army had to have supplies. If none arrived, there was only one way to keep the men alive. This was to spread them over a wide area so that they could live on the rather scanty food stores in the towns, villages and farms. Scattered in this way an army could not fight a battle, or resist the enemy. Fortunately for Wellington his supplies were far better organised than those of the French. This meant he could keep his army together longer than they could, which explains much of his success.

This does not mean that the English supply service was perfect. This service was called the Commissariat, and the men in charge of it were called Commissaries. Too many of them tried to make money on the side. Since Commissaries were fond of putting their stores into churches—this was the only convenient place in many Spanish villages—someone joked, 'My house shall be called the house of prayer, but ye have made it a den of thieves.' Not only were some commissaries dishonest, but, like all of us, they could make mistakes. You will see in a later chapter how one of them, through selfishness and stupidity, cost the army more lives and hardship than a battle would have done.

Nearly everything the army used came from overseas. Without the Royal Navy and the merchant fleet, Wellington could have done nothing. The ships took most of the stores to Lisbon. From there, every few days, a convoy of mules and ox-carts set out for the front. Most of the *muleteers* were ruffians. This is what an English officer said about them:

'These muleteers are very numerous. They receive a *dollar* daily for each beast and their rations extra. The more buttons a muleteer can sew on his waistcoat and trowsers, the finer he is

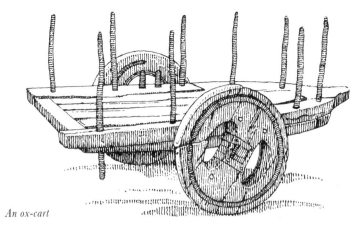

An ox-cart

dressed in his own opinion. They drink the liquors entrusted to their conveyance and fill up the vacancy with salt water—a nauseous beverage. They are so accustomed to the jogging of the beasts and the beasts are so used to the nodding of their riders that they both sleep and ride and walk together. On the long journeys they sleep under hedges and down the ditches. When riding along through quags and bogs, over heaths and through forests pitch dark, I've frequently heard these people discoursing among the brambles and thickets. We are always prepared

Muleteers

for action as they carry short *carbines* as well as long knives and are notorious thieves and murderers.'

But without the muleteers the army would have starved. This is what William Tomkinson said:

'The system, though expensive, was excellent, and the army continued its operations in countries where there was nothing to be had, and where any other army without mules could not have remained. Our advance from the lines in 1811, through a country completely exhausted, was most wonderful. The enemy were quite astonished how we got on.'

But sometimes the mule trains did not arrive. Private Wheeler once had to make a long march without supplies:

'We were in the midst of a desert, a very long march in front and no hope of getting any more bread until we could gain some place where some Commissariat was stationed; thus circumstanced it required all the art of Colonel Mainwaring to keep up our drooping spirits. One day he halted us, called the Quarter Master, took out a letter and said he had received the welcome news, bread was at hand. The Quarter Master was to ride forward and purchase enough to last the regiment a week. We then continued our march till night, stretching our necks and making the best use of our eyes at every turn of the road to see if we could catch a glimpse of the Quarter Master. It was all a delusion. At length we turned off the road and encamped for the night; in the morning the Colonel wondered where the Quarter Master could be. He was confident that bread was at no great distance, for he could smell it; it could not be far off. At this moment the Quarter Master appeared with a loaf. The Colonel held it up saying, "I knew I was right. My nose never deceived me; there is plenty of this only two leagues distant; come let us away to the feast" '

The 'feast' was half a ration of *biscuit*, rum and beef. It was another three days before the men had their bread.

10 The Medical Services

The man in charge of these services was called the Inspector General of the Medical Department. From 1811 onwards a Sir James McGrigor held this post. He had been an army doctor for a long time, and he was hard-working and efficient.

There was always work for McGrigor and his doctors. A battle, of course, gave them enormous problems. This is what one soldier found in a churchyard after a battle:

'Two long tables had been procured and were placed end to end among the graves and upon them were laid the men whose limbs it was found necessary to amputate. Both French and English were constantly lifted on and off these tables. As soon as the operation was performed upon one lot, they were carried off, and those in waiting hoisted up; the surgeons with their sleeves turned up, and their hands and arms covered with blood, looked like butchers in the shambles. I saw as I passed at least twenty legs lying on the ground.'

This is what McGrigor himself found in Central Spain after the Battle of Salamanca:

'At several places on my route I found considerable numbers of sick. Some of them were left by the parties of recruits proceeding to the army, who had fallen ill in the long march from Lisbon; many others had been left sick by the divisions of the army on their march from Salamanca to Madrid. The causes of the diseases of the greater part of the soldiers were dissipation and drunkenness, but not a few officers were likewise sick at those places. Some of them had been wounded at the battle of Salamanca, and would not be restrained from proceeding to the Spanish capital. The situation of some of these parties was most deplorable. Not only without medicine and medical attention, but also without provision of any kind, many of them were sinking in the last stage of disease, and not a few had died without having been seen by a medical man. I everywhere went round and visited them but was powerless to help.'

A great battle, as you can see, strewed the countryside with human wrecks, and the army just did not have enough doctors to help them.

Even without a battle there were problems enough. The troops marched great distances, carrying heavy loads. They slept out in all weathers; they might be without proper food for days together. Sometimes the army would have to camp for a long time in unhealthy, swampy country. Sometimes there would be an outbreak of a dangerous infectious disease, such as typhus. All in all, sickness and disease killed far more men than the French.

There were no proper hospitals. The doctors took over churches and monasteries, and these were often overcrowded and filthy. Moreover, the army was often many miles from its hospitals and a man who was wounded or sick would have a long journey to the rear. Those who could walk staggered back as best they could. The rest travelled by ox-cart, as you can see from the cartoon opposite. This man is lucky. He is an officer, so he has a cart to himself.

Of course many of the sick and wounded died before they even reached hospital.

The ordinary army doctors were a mixed bunch. It was difficult to persuade good doctors to join the army. Those who did found it difficult to go on with their studies. There were too many distractions, and it was only too easy to join the other officers, particularly in their drinking parties. McGrigor himself preferred tea to wine, and when bound by good manners to go to a party he usually asked an *orderly* to come along with a message that he was urgently needed at the hospital. It was not long before the other officers grew wise to this, and when the message arrived the cry would go up, 'Oh, oh! Is the Doctor's tea ready?'

We will now see what it was like to be a wounded soldier. William Tomkinson was wounded soon after he arrived in

Wounded officer going sick to the rear

Portugal in 1809. He tells us how it happened:

'I was in the act of firing my pistol at the head of a French infantry man, when my arm dropped, without any power on my part to raise it. The next thing I recollect was my horse galloping in an ungovernable manner amongst this body of infantry, with both my hands hanging down, though I do not recollect being shot in the left arm. In this state one of their bayonets was stuck into him, and he, fortunately, turned round. He went full gallop to the rear and on coming to a fence he selected a low place under a tree, knocked my head into it, when I fell off him.'

Tomkinson was knocked unconscious. He woke up to find a Frenchman helping him to the edge of the field, where he propped him against a wall. Then some Germans in our own army came along, but so far from helping him, they went through his pockets and stole everything worth having. Fortunately his servant now arrived and he had a chance to look at his wounds. He had been shot in the neck and in both arms. Also there was a curious wound in his left elbow that looked like a bayonet thrust. He had also been struck in the chest, but fortunately this was only a glancing blow, though it was some hours before he could breathe properly.

47

He was carried on a door to a village where his wounds were bound up, but even now he was not safe from plunderers. A peasant stole the brass buttons from his coat. Also the shock was now beginning to tell, for he had a high temperature and became *delirious*. When he had recovered a little he had to go to Oporto. It was about six miles away over a rough track. He wrote:

'They wanted me to travel on a common bullock cart, drawn by two oxen at the rate of about two miles per hour; the wheels are made of solid pieces of wood, very low, fixed to the axle tree which turns round and from the friction the noise may be heard to a great distance. Not infrequently the wheels are not round, and give a jerk in every circle they make.'

Fortunately Tomkinson was able to have a Sedan chair. This was much more comfortable, but he was very irritable from his suffering and ordered his servant to shoot the next Portuguese who lifted the curtains of the chair to look at him. At Oporto they put him to bed and ordered him not to move. He was in pain enough from his wounds, but now he developed bed sores and the mosquitoes buzzing round nearly drove him mad. His left hand was so painful that he could not even allow his servant to wash away the blood that had clotted all over it.

Then he had some luck. Something in his left elbow worked its way to the surface. The surgeon opened the elbow and to his amazement pulled out a button. It had not been a bayonet wound after all. The ball which struck him a glancing blow on the chest had taken off the button and driven it into his arm. He said that when the button came out: 'The relief was instantaneous. I moved all my fingers immediately, and was employed the whole day in putting my hand in hot water and getting off the clotted blood.'

Slowly Tomkinson began to recover. He spent his time playing cards with his servant or singing songs. As he was in the house of a Portuguese Viscount he had plenty of good food and wine. Animals and insects now bothered him at their peril. The cats of Oporto kept him awake at night, so that in the daytime he shot at them with his pistols when they came on the roof of the house opposite. Six weeks after he was wounded he was able to sail for England, but it was a full year before he came back to the Peninsula ready for service.

William Tomkinson was a brave man, but from that time onwards he had a dread of lying wounded on the battlefield, particularly when he watched fire sweeping through dry grass, or saw eagles and vultures circling in the sky.

Private Wheeler was shot in the leg during a battle in 1813. The fighting swayed backwards and forwards. Twice French troops passed over him, and twice British troops. As the French finally retreated one of their soldiers robbed him. Wheeler was furious: 'As soon as the enemy had passed I put my hand on a firelock. I had not taken my eye off the fellow who robbed me. I took deadly aim at him and down he fell. I was so overjoyed that, forgetting the danger, I sat up with my cap on the muzzle of my firelock and cheered my comrades as they passed me.'

Wheeler then crawled to the man who had robbed him, took his money back and went to have his wound dressed. He then made his way to a farm. Here he went into a barn in which the French had kept their stores. It was now full of wounded. 'Brandy had made them forget their trouble. Those who had received wounds in the legs were sitting down smoking and drinking and either listening or joining in chorus to some war song. Others who had the use of their legs, some of whom with their heads wrapped in bandages, and some with their arms in slings, were footing it to the merry dance.' Wheeler did not join this rabble, but limped over to the farm house.

When his wound was nearly better he went by sea to a convalescent hospital. This journey was an adventure in itself. The little ship ran into fog and high seas. The wounded were flung about and found themselves sitting in sea water. The Spanish captain blamed Wheeler. He had lit his pipe at the lamp that burned in front of a statue of the Virgin. The wind had blown out the candle and at once the bad weather had begun. Several of the wounded died during the voyage.

Those who lived settled down in the convalescent hospital, but Wheeler's troubles were not over. He had been wounded in November. In April his wound broke out again. It began to throb and was so badly infected that he had to be moved to the ward for incurables. This was a grim place. While Wheeler was there five men died one after the other in the next bed. The wounded leg had wasted away to skin and bone and he was told he would have to have it cut off. However there was a little Spanish doctor helping in the hospital. 'He brought from his house a small bottle filled with something like pepper and salt mixed; with this he covered the wound, on which he put lint, bandaged it up, crossed himself, muttered something and left me.'

Next day most of the poison came away with the lint, and the wound began to heal again. But eleven months after he had been wounded, Wheeler was writing home to say it would be a long time before he could return to his duty. He was, of course, lucky that the Spanish doctor found him. In the hands of British doctors he would have lost his leg first and then, probably, his life.

11   Life in the Army

The Army on the March

The army did more marching than anything else. With its long trains of mules, its ox-carts doing just over two miles an hour, and its guns, it could not move far in a day. Nine or ten miles would be normal, though, if pressed, it could do over thirty. But these small distances, day after day, meant that the men covered enormous distances in the course of the year.

The soldier's day usually began an hour and a half before dawn. The bugles sounded and the men roused themselves grumbling and cursing. They loaded their haversacks, rolled their blankets, and made their way to their alarm posts. The alarm post was the place they were supposed to go if there was an enemy attack. It was also the parade ground. Meanwhile the camp followers were loading the baggage animals and the ox-carts, and the gunners were harnessing their teams. The Provost Marshal went his rounds and when every company had reported 'All present', the order was given 'By sections of threes, march!'

It would now be the grey light of early dawn. The troops marched as if on a parade with their muskets at the slope. But soon they would have the order 'March at ease'. This meant they could sling their firelocks over their shoulders and talk or joke with their friends.

The first halt came after half an hour when each man would eat a biscuit and a piece of meat for breakfast. They would adjust their loads so that they sat comfortably on their backs. Thereafter the army halted every hour, each halt lasting just over five minutes.

Marching conditions could be very different. In the heat of

Serjeant and private of infantry in Winter marching order

summer the troops raised dust clouds, their throats were dry and it was difficult to find water in central Spain. In spring or autumn it could be bitterly cold, or wet. The army did not often move in winter, but it was by no means unknown. It is not surprising that there were stragglers. A man might be unwell; he might be overcome by the heat, or the weight of his sixty pound load; he might twist his ankle. If things went wrong, he would have to fall out. Provided his excuse was genuine, his captain would give him a ticket. A man caught straggling without a ticket was in trouble. A soldier who fell out usually managed to catch up again at the next halt. He was anxious to do this, as the two other men in his file had to carry his pack and musket. He would be none too popular if he stayed away longer than he had to.

Provided the enemy was a long way off the Quarter Master would go ahead of the division. If they were to spend the night in a town, he would divide up the place so that the various companies would know where they had to go as soon as they arrived. But generally they slept out in the open. The general would choose the camp site, remembering to guard against enemy attack, and to find a place where they could get wood for fires and fresh water. As with the town, the Quarter Master would divide up the camping ground, so that each company had its own spot. When the troops arrived, the general saw to it that the camp was protected by a string of outposts. If there were cavalry to the front he would make contact with them. As they arrived, each company would line up on its alarm post. They would then be shown their section of the camp ground and would fall out to eat and make themselves as comfortable as they could.

The Bivouac

A bivouac is a camp made without tents. The army did not have tents until 1813. First of all the men would pile their arms, then each captain would order his company, 'Fall out and make yourselves comfortable for the night.' Under reasonable conditions good soldiers could 'make themselves comfortable for the night'. Some of them went to draw rations, others went for water, and others made fires. Trees were a great help. They gave shelter and firewood. The troops hung their spare clothing and equipment in the branches: they might, if they had time, cut enough wood to make themselves huts. Otherwise they could make a barricade of saddles, baggage and haversacks, and sit with this behind them and a blazing fire in front.

The first bivouac was quite an experience for a soldier. John Kincaid found his rations were 'a mouldy biscuit and a pound of

Soldiers in camp

beef", and his baggage mule was miles to the rear. Through the night he woke up from time to time, uncomfortably cold, and soaked with dew. He then jumped about until he got 'a sleeping quantity of warmth', and dozed off again.

In addition to the wet and cold there were the strange night noises and insects and animals. William Tomkinson was kept awake by croaking frogs; there might be grasshoppers, or lizards or snakes might slide over a sleeping man. One of the donkeys with the army might start a braying 'which is instantly taken up by every mule and donkey in the army, and sent echoing from regiment to regiment, over hill and valley until it dies away in the distance'.

One night some store bullocks strayed among the piles of arms and hit them flying. The clatter of the falling muskets made the bullocks stampede over the sleeping soldiers. The baggage horses joined in and the cry went up that French cavalry were attacking. The camp followers fled. A woman from the 52nd ran several miles and swore, 'that as God was her judge, she did not leave her regiment until she saw the last man of them cut to pieces'.

Officers were more comfortable than the men. They had their own servants, and they helped one another by eating in small groups, each called a 'mess'. They took it in turn to get the food. Kincaid says the man on duty, 'goes to the regimental butcher and *bespeaks* a portion of the only purchaseable commodities—hearts, liver and kidneys: and also to see if he can *do* the commissary out of a few extra biscuits or a canteen of brandy'.

When dinner was ready, they all came along with their *haversacks*, each of which should contain 'a couple of biscuits, a sausage, a little tea and sugar, a knife, fork and spoon, a tin cup (which answers to the name of tea-cup, soup-plate, wine-glass and tumbler), and half a dozen cigars'.

For bedding, each man had his blanket and great coat. They might sew their blankets to make sleeping bags, or two men might lie down together and share their bedding. A veteran would now sleep soundly. Not rain, nor frost, nor insects, nor braying donkeys would wake him now.

'Habit', says Kincaid, 'gives endurance, and fatigue is the best night-cap.' Only one thing would disturb him and that was the bugle. 'The first note puts the soldier on his legs like lightning: when, muttering a few curses at the unreasonableness of the hour, he plants himself on his alarm post, without knowing or caring about the cause.'

In good weather, it was not too bad to bivouac. Tomkinson describes how he and Major Cocks lived in Portugal in 1810: 'Cocks and myself had nothing with us but a change of linen, a pot to boil potatoes, and the same to make coffee in, with a frying pan. We never wanted for a single article, excepting wheat bread, which failed us occasionally. We could always march in five minutes, never slept out of our clothes and never enjoyed better health. Half past two in the morning was the hour we got up.'

But if summer in Portugal was one thing, a rainy autumn on the mountains of central Spain was quite another. We hear of troops having to bivouac during torrential rain in fields ankle deep in water, or on ground churned up by the army, so that it was knee deep in mud. All that you could do was to spread branches and lie on them in the hope that they would keep you from sinking too deeply into the mire. All in all, the troops were much happier when they had their tents in 1813.

The Billet

A billet is a private house in which a soldier finds lodging. While on the march the troops usually had to make do with bivouacs, but during the worst part of the winter the army would scatter over a wide area and the men would find themselves sharing Portuguese or Spanish houses with their owners. They were not always welcome guests.

John Kincaid tells two stories of families who did not want him. At one house a woman told him she had a sick daughter upstairs. Kincaid said he was a doctor and promised he would cure the girl. This he did by giving her a sharp smack on the bottom. Another time a sour-faced woman gave him a dirty old attic, but Kincaid found a pleasant room vacant downstairs and insisted on having it. He returned that night to find a fat friar in his room snoring loudly. Kincaid knew what to do. He picked him up by the ears 'and before he had time to get himself broad awake, had chucked him and his clothing and bedding out at the door'. The next morning he saw his hostess lurking by a window—and he was careful not to walk under it.

Through a long winter, soldiers and civilians could easily irritate one another. One difficulty was that whereas most of Wellington's men were Protestants, the Spaniards and Portuguese were Catholics. In fact, the only people in our army that the Spaniards and Portuguese really liked were the Irish because, of course, they too were Catholics. Private Wheeler makes it clear he thought his hosts were a superstitious lot: 'The fire was always occupied by the female part of the family. The mistress, an old shrivelled hag who has been smoke dried some sixty winters and would be a fit character for one of the witches in Macbeth, places herself on the right. Next to her are seated her three lovely daughters, real *brunettes*, with eyes as black as sloes. Then the servants complete the group. Thus huddled together, each having their string of beads and crosses to charm the devil from them, they relate some horrid tale of slaughtered friend by the enemy, or of some headless ghost, till their fears are worked to such a pitch that the least noise frightens them out of what little sense they have.'

Not only did Wheeler dislike their superstitions; he wanted to sit by the fire. So he took a packet of gunpowder and dropped it among the embers. A jet of flame shot into the air and the women fled screaming.

Portuguese houses were not luxurious. Wheeler's house had three storeys, the first of which was for animals. It was always full of smoke. There were no beds for the Englishmen, so they had to make themselves comfortable as best they could. Wheeler made himself a pile of dry fern and used his knapsack for a pillow. He put his legs in the sleeves of an old coat, tied at the ends and pulled his trousers on top of that. He goes on: 'My red jacket has the distinguished place of covering my seat of honour and lastly my blanket covers all. In this manner I have slept as comfortable as a prince.'

An officer's billet

His visitors at night

Spain and Portugal were poor countries. Almost everything the army needed, it had to carry along with it. Some of the food and equipment went in carts. You can see a picture of one of these on page 43. Such a cart is heavy and difficult to move— $2\frac{1}{2}$ miles an hour would be about the best it could do. The axle turned with the wheels and made a squeak which, Kincaid said, made the noise of a knife edge being scraped on a plate sound like music.

Most of the things, however, were carried by mules. Each company had one to carry its camp kettles and in each battalion there was one for the *entrenching tools,* one for the paymaster's books and one for the surgeon's medical *panniers.*

The officers had many more animals. William Tomkinson brought his charger, Bob, from England and then in Lisbon he says, 'I bought an English mare and two ponies; the latter for luggage.'

Kincaid says: 'The officers of each company had a Portuguese boy in charge of a donkey on whom their little comforts depended. He carried our *boat cloaks* and blankets, was provided with a small pig skin for wine, a canteen for spirits, a small quantity of tea and sugar, a goat tied to the donkey, and two or three dollars in his pocket for the purchase of bread, butter or any other luxury.' No one asked the boy where the supplies came from—but he was in trouble if he did not produce any.

Looking after these animals was no fun for the officers' servants. Private Wheeler was a batman for a while and he hated it. His captain's mule was called Betty, and she often gave trouble, particularly one day when Wheeler had to load her while under fire, 'Fortunately for me, old Betty stood fire very well and I got her loaded without much trouble. Some others were not so fortunate, their animals ran about half loaded. Some animals would be knocked down, then a shot would dab in amongst a heap of boxes and scatter their contents around the place. I was moving off, speaking very kindly to old Betty, then cursing the French, when a shot dropped in front of my mule, and sent her a-kicking, and away went load, saddle and all between her legs.'

Buying these animals was as risky as buying a secondhand car. Kincaid bought what looked to be a sound mule. He was disappointed. At the end of the first day's march he found his animal had a broken jaw bone and it was almost impossible to feed him. Another time his servant thought he would be rather clever and changed a small but good baggage horse for one that was much bigger. This horse ate so much that he needed all his strength to carry his own fodder. Kincaid put him on half rations and he became so thin that his bones stuck out. He says: 'I could easily have hung my hat on any part of his hind quarters.' When the army arrived at Madrid in 1812, Kincaid gave the horse a rest, fattened him up and exchanged him for a mule and five dollars. He went on: 'I expended the first dollar the next day, in getting admission to a bull fight, where the first thing that met my astonished eyes was a mad bull giving the finishing prod to my unfortunate big horse.'

Advance Guard Work

When an army was on the move the main body, strung out along the road with all its baggage and camp followers, could not easily defend itself. There had to be an advance guard.

How was the advance guard made up? There were usually cavalry, infantry and artillery, but, so that they could move quickly, they were all light troops—light infantry, light cavalry and light horse artillery. If it was close country with lots of walls and other obstacles then the light infantry would go forward. On the other hand, in the plains, it was the light cavalry that had the honour. The horse artillery had valuable guns, so they never led an advance, but were usually near at hand, in case they were needed.

As he was in the Light Dragoons, William Tomkinson saw a lot of advance guard work. He had a particularly exciting time while Wellington was following Massena out of Portugal in 1811. The French were demoralised and it was easy to round up stragglers. Tomkinson says: 'I fell in with five infantry with a flock of goats and nine asses. On our coming up they surrendered. I then fell in with thirteen infantry under a serjeant, escorting two mules laden with Indian corn. They at first seemed inclined to fire, cocking their muskets; but on our riding up, laid them down without a shot.'

A serjeant in his regiment was out with four troopers when he saw an enemy picket with arms piled. He thought that if he rushed them, he could reach the muskets before they did. He was wrong. The enemy met him with a volley and one of his men fell wounded. He decided it was too late to turn back and charged on. With his three surviving troopers he took forty prisoners.

The problem was often what to do with prisoners who lay down and refused to move. This happened to Tomkinson, and all he could do was leave the man behind. According to the rules of war he was entitled to kill the man, but he could not bring himself to do this in cold blood.

The Rearguard

A rearguard was made up like an advance guard, with cavalry, infantry and artillery. But being in the rear is quite a different feeling. Soldiers soon lose heart when they have to retreat. Tomkinson describes what happened one day when his regiment was rather late in moving off. 'The country is as much enclosed as possible, only one road to retire by; the enemy's cavalry and infantry close up engaged with our skirmishers. We first walked, then trotted and at last galloped, our rear was much pressed, and obliged to halt and charge them in the lane. Nothing ever appeared worse, both to ourselves and the enemy, as they must have seen our confusion.'

However, the enemy did not have it all his own way. Tomkinson describes the rescue of some guns surprised by the enemy in the narrow streets of a village. The French cavalry had crossed a bridge and half of them had turned a corner when the light dragoons charged. 'They instantly went about and wished to retire. There was the greatest noise and confusion with the enemy, their front wishing to get away and their rear, not knowing what was going on, stood still. We took twelve and killed six, driving them over the bridge again, and by this means allowing time for the guns that remained in the town to get clear away.'

Pickets

When the army halted it sent pickets forward. A picket is a body of soldiers who keep an eye on the enemy, report on his movements and give warning if there is an attack. In each picket there would be about thirty or forty men. The officer in charge would divide them into two groups. One group would go forward singly or in pairs and take up good positions to keep watch. These men were called *videttes*. The other half of the picket would rest, and every two hours the two groups would change places.

Pickets were made up of light troops, cavalry or infantry. They had to be always ready to move. Cavalrymen did not unsaddle their horses and slept with their bridles in their hands. As dawn was the most dangerous time, they all stood to arms an hour before daybreak and kept on the alert until there was enough light to see a grey horse a mile away.

Pickets usually had a system of field signals. A Captain Blakeney tells us he made his videttes take two smooth stones with them. Each man struck his stones together twice slowly and the signal passed along the line. If any vidette failed to do this for more than five minutes, then the next man struck his stones three times quickly. This message would go back to the picket and someone would go out to have a look. In this way a sentry could not sleep for more than five minutes. Tomkinson describes signals given in daylight by his troopers. If the enemy advanced, the vidette put his cap on his carbine; if he saw cavalry, he circled slowly to the left; if he saw infantry, he circled slowly to the right. If the enemy were coming on quickly, he cantered round in a tight circle. All this seems to show that pickets were well organised. So they were, much of the time— but not always.

One lieutenant took fright because his relief videttes did not return. He at once reported that the French were advancing, and threw the whole Light Division into confusion. Shortly afterwards the videttes came in—they had only lost their way.

A certain Lieutenant Wheatley found himself in even worse trouble. His men became drunk and Wheatley had to stand sentry himself all night. A worse shock came in the morning for one of the men was missing. After a long search they found him stripped naked and frozen to death. It seemed now that the Colonel would learn what had happened, but the punishment for sleeping on duty was death. Wheatley says: 'I determined to screen the poor fellows. So digging a deep hole we buried the man and I reported him as having deserted to the enemy. The other three would go to the Devil for me now, but should it be discovered, I shall go to him myself, I fear.'

Sometimes nothing happened. Kincaid says he and his men lay four months near the enemy and neither side fired a shot. Sometimes there was a false alarm. One night a vidette saw a man moving suspiciously out in front. When his relief came he advised him to watch this suspicious character carefully. In the daylight they were both amused to find the man was just a bush blowing backwards and forwards. William Tomkinson was alarmed one day by a lot of activity among the enemy. It looked as if they were preparing a big attack. But he says: 'It was nothing more than the enemy's generals visiting their outposts which may be a pleasant ride for them, though if they would not move their troops it would save us much unnecessary trouble.'

Tomkinson was not above taking his revenge. He would sometimes launch a mock attack on the enemy outposts and withdraw as soon as they lit their beacon, knowing that he had roused the French army for nothing at all.

Although it was strictly forbidden, troops sometimes talked with enemy videttes. Captain Blakeney often got himself some wine this way. The Frenchman would place his flask on the ground and withdraw. Blakeney then went up, filled his canteen and withdrew in his turn. He could not explain why two men who could talk together as friends, would not touch one another at any price.

There is an extraordinary story of a French and British sentry who became friends. The Frenchman wanted to go back to his camp for something he had forgotten, so the Englishman took his place. He had his own musket on one shoulder, the Frenchman's on the other and he stood keeping watch for both armies! But usually picket duty was serious enough. William

Tomkinson describes how the French rushed his picket. You will see that he saved his men by quick thinking and an intelligent piece of deduction:

'The enemy this morning half an hour before daylight, passed the ford with two hundred cavalry as an advance, driving in my picket at a gallop; they were close at our heels for two miles, we firing as much as we could to give the other pickets notice, and cutting at them as they came up to us. I had seen a light go down their line as if they were counting men in their ranks, on the opposite side of the river. I had mounted my men (which was fortunate) as they came on at a gallop, and I had some difficulty in getting all away.'

Finally, here is a dreadful account of a night on picket duty. The writer is John Kincaid. This happened during Masséna's retreat from Portugal in 1811 when the villages were full of Portuguese too weak from starvation to move.

'Our post that night was one of terrific grandeur. The hills behind were in a blaze of light with the British camp-fires, as were those in our front with the French ones. Both hills were abrupt and lofty, not above eight hundred yards *asunder*, and we were in the burning village between. The roofs of houses were every instant falling in, and the sparks and the flames were ascending to the clouds. The streets were strewed with the dying and dead. Some had been murdered and some killed in action, which, together with the half-famished wretches whom we had saved from burning, contributed in making it a scene which was well calculated to shake a stout heart.'

One vidette went mad. He came running in to swear that six dead Frenchmen were advancing on him with hatchets over their shoulders.

Amusements

Spain and Portugal provided few amusements—most of the time the soldiers made their own. We hear of the soldiers racing, playing cricket and football and boxing. Sometimes they felt like something a little different and would have a donkey race. In this the rider sat facing the tail while his partner

63

ran ahead waving a bunch of carrots at the donkey. Another good sport was chasing a greasy pig. The winner was the man who caught the pig, and as his prize, he kept it.

The officers had more choice than the men. Most of them were country gentlemen and could not do without their favourite sport of hunting. In the Peninsula they found hares, partridges and foxes. They had their horses with them, so the only problem was dogs and these they had sent out from England. Wellington had a pack of hounds by 1811, and it was not long before there was one in each division. Wellington's remark about one of his officers shows how important he thought hunting was: 'I hope we shall soon have Waters again. He has been very near dying, poor fellow, and what is worse, I heard he lost all his dogs.'

Sometimes there was dancing—often under difficult conditions. One ball took place in a room that had lost part of its roof. There was an unsightly hole in the floor which they covered with a carpet and then posted a sentry near it to stop people falling through. So bored were the officers in winter that they would go to a lot of trouble to attend a dance. William Tomkinson walked nine miles in mid-February to attend a ball, climbing he said, 'over the steepest and highest hills I ever passed'.

John Kincaid liked dancing. He wrote: 'We invited the villagers, every evening, to a dance at our quarters. We used to flourish away at the *bolero, fandango* and waltz, and wound up early in the morning with a supper of roasted chestnuts.'

He also approved of the Spanish girls: 'A Spanish peasant girl has an *address* about her which I have never met with in the same class of any other country: as she at once enters into society with the ease and confidence of one who has been accustomed to it all her life.'

Perhaps William Tomkinson was more fussy, or less fortunate. Anyway he wrote with disgust after a ball at Salamanca: 'We had heard much of Spanish beauty: Salamanca, I fancy, is an exception to the rest of Spain.'

English troops did not like bull fights. The men of the 16th Light Dragoons found a good chance to make fun of this sport when the Spaniards promised them a bull fight, but could find neither bull nor *matador*. The troopers went to the commissary and borrowed a store bullock.

'A poor footsore beast', said Tomkinson, 'he had marched several leagues that morning and had more the appearance of dying than coming to grace so gay a scene. A *farrier* took off his apron and flapped it at the animal and two or three dragoons joined in and pushed him around a bit. Then they sent him back to the commissary and the poor thing was killed and eaten that same night.'

Plunder

Generally speaking troops were not supposed to plunder. Wellington was very strict about this. Nevertheless plundering did go on. There was a good number of criminals in the army and they had not left their thieving habits at home.

One form of plundering was lawful. This was taking things, within reason, from the enemy. Even an officer could take a horse. John Kincaid took an officer prisoner at Badajoz and he says, 'His handsome black mare became my charger during the remainder of the war.'

The common soldiers went over the dead, robbing and stripping them after a battle. Kincaid sometimes helped bury

Stripping the dead

the dead and says, 'I never saw the body of one with a rag on after a battle.' He had a narrow escape himself once, for the men did not mind whether they plundered their own people or the enemy. He saw some troops moving into danger and rushed forward to save them. A musket ball struck him a glancing blow and he fell unconscious. When he came to himself he found his coat undone—one of the men he had saved had started to strip him. The fellow had run away from the enemy, and, Kincaid said, he was thankful for the French advance or he would have lost his coat and his trousers along with it.

Unlike robbing the enemy and the dead, taking food and drink from the Portuguese and Spaniards was illegal, but it went on. An entry in Tomkinson's diary reads: 'Headquarters of the army came to Villa Verde. The place is famed for a light white wine. The village is quite hollow with large wine vaults. The men cannot be kept out of them.'

It was only too common for the enemy to advance and find drunken English soldiers straggling from their units, quite unable to fight or even to run away. One day a group of these revellers had a shock. Tomkinson says: 'The men, after drinking nearly to the bottom of one of the wine casks, looked into it and saw a dead peasant who had been put in by the French.'

There was perhaps more justification in taking food, especially during a retreat when anything left by the British would fall into the hands of the French. A Major Roberts in Private Wheeler's brigade even encouraged his men to take food from the fields. One day he saw one of his men in charge of the Provost Marshal, who had arrested him for stealing potatoes. Roberts promised to punish the thief himself and took him away. Wheeler says, 'The Major gave Jack a good lecture for being so foolish as to be caught. He ordered him to be released, "Go to my servant and get your *murphys*. I have only taken a few for my dinner."'

Even William Tomkinson once shared plundered food, and he was always very correct. He says: 'My old dragoon had got me a turkey as he passed on the march. He had plucked it coming along, and on my return from seeing the men, I found him holding it in the flame of the fire by legs and wings at a time. He had no wood and broke up some cane-bottomed chairs for the purpose of making a fire. I rather reproached him, and the only answer I got was that I should find the turkey very good: we soon finished it.'

This was while Wellington was retreating to Lisbon in the autumn of 1810. Conditions were very bad and there was every excuse for depriving the French of the turkey, and the chairs.

Since most of the time the soldiers lived on tough stringy beef they were very fond of poultry. Captain Blakeney found some men in his regiment who were experts at animal noises. He came into a farmhouse one day and found a man crowing like a cockerel. He asked him what he was doing and had the mysterious reply, 'I believe we have them, sir.' Soon there was an answering crow from behind a locked door. The soldiers made the farmer open it and out came a cock and several hens.

One day Tomkinson was amused to see a man attempting to fight the French with a haversack of food on his back, a live turkey on one side of his cloak, and two hens on the other.

Apart from taking wine and food there was little enough looting, save on two memorable occasions. One was after the fall of Badajoz, which you will read about in chapter 12 and the other was after the battle of Vittoria in 1813.

At Vittoria, King Joseph was escaping into France with all the plunder he and his followers had taken from the Spaniards over several years. His army broke and fled, and his magnificent baggage train fell into the hands of the British. One man found a table laid with silver plate, all ready for dinner. He picked up the four corners of the table-cloth and swept the whole lot into camp. Others found oil paintings, furniture and expensive clothes; others again found food and drink. The luckiest were those who found the treasure chests, and gold and silver coins worth over two million pounds went into their pockets. There were then soldiers who had goods and others who had money, so the camp became a market. Wheeler says: 'The market soon changed into a general maskerade. British soldiers were to be seen in French generals' uniforms, covered with stars and military orders, others had attired themselves in female dresses, richly embroidered in gold and silver.'

As usual when this sort of thing happens, it was the scoundrels in the army who had the most. One colonel was disgusted. His battalion had behaved themselves, and none of his men had anything. He determined to reward them. Fortunately some chests had been saved from the plunderers; they were very heavy and the colonel was sure they held something valuable. The troops paraded for their reward, and the chests were broken open. They were full of horseshoe nails.

Discipline

To understand the problem of discipline, we must remember that many of Wellington's men were criminals, or near criminals. They were not easy to rule, and most officers, including Wellington, thought that only savage laws and savage punishments could keep order.

What crimes did the soldiers commit? Fairly common and very serious was desertion. There was a steady trickle of deserters between the two armies—Frenchmen coming over to our army, and our own people going over to the enemy. The reasons for desertion were many. Tomkinson says two men deserted when Masséna's army was near Lisbon in 1810. They thought the town was bound to fall, and felt they would like to join in the plunder. Unhappily for them, no one had told them about the lines of Torres Vedras. Some other men Tomkinson speaks of were a couple who had plundered a chapel. They fled rather than face a *court martial*. Probably the most common reason for deserting was that a man had stood all he could bear. He had perhaps been sleeping outside in all weathers for weeks, half starved, his pay long in arrears. He could not but believe things were better in the enemy camp, and went over to relieve, so he hoped, his misery.

Naturally loyal troops hated deserters more than the enemy.

Stealing was all too common. This could range from robbery with violence, down to taking a few potatoes from a field. You have already read about this, in the section on plunder.

Possibly the most common offence was being drunk. Sir James McGrigor said: 'One day, I am sure, I saw five hundred men at least in a state of beastly intoxication. All subordination was gone, all alike, English, Scots and Irish were equally the slaves of drunkenness. Had the enemy come upon us at the time, we should have been an easy prey to him.'

Of course, it was no crime to be a little tipsy round the camp fire after a long day's march, or in your billet miles from the enemy. But to be drunk, for example, on sentry duty, was quite another matter.

Punishments were execution by hanging or shooting, or flogging. Hanging was grim enough to see. When he came to Portugal John Kincaid 'saw an English and a Portuguese soldier dangling by the boughs of a tree—the first example I had ever seen of martial law'. Execution by firing squad was even more horrible. The whole battalion had to watch. First of all the sentence of the court martial was read. Then the chaplain had a few words with the condemned man. His eyes were bound, and the firing party watched the Provost Marshal. They presented their muskets and fired on a signal from him. After the execution the battalion marched past the corpse.

Hanging was usually the punishment for robbery or murder. Shooting was for desertion. Almost all other crimes were punished by flogging. This was a grisly business, and once again the whole battalion had to watch. The sentences varied from 25 to 1,200 strokes. Anything around a thousand lashes was much the same as a sentence of death.

It is a relief to know that some officers did what they could to avoid flogging their men. Private Wheeler's first commanding officer, Colonel Mainwaring was usually lenient. One man who had been sentenced to 500 strokes was cut down after 75. Instead of the balance of the flogging the Colonel made the criminal walk between the ranks and ordered the men 'to spit on the cowardly *poltroon*'. Some units managed without flogging at all. Unhappily there were others where beatings were too frequent and too brutal.

One thing that seems very unfair was that there was quite a different code of rules for officers. The worst an officer had to fear was being cashiered—that is being dismissed in disgrace. This would be for dishonesty or flagrant disobedience. Less serious was suspension of pay and rank, usually for three or six months. This might be for neglect of duty, such as allowing the troops to pull down houses for firewood, or going absent without leave. For a slight offence, such as striking a soldier, the officer would be reprimanded in front of the entire regiment. Needless to say, if a soldier struck an officer, he would be severely flogged or even executed.

The officer responsible for much of the discipline of the army was the Provost Marshal. Among other things he had the right to punish a man without trial if he actually saw him committing an offence. The men hated and feared this officer. One day Private Wheeler came to the house of a badly frightened farmer. There were drunken soldiers all around and the farmer begged Wheeler to protect him. Wheeler took a piece of chalk and wrote on the door 'Provost Marshal'. 'This', he says, 'was the complete *talisman*: the house was spellbound against marauders.'

Women with the Army

In each company about five men were allowed to bring their wives overseas. They drew lots to choose the lucky ones.

These women were a rough, unruly lot. Some of them were stronger than the men. One Irishwoman saved her husband

Soldiers and their wives on the march

from the French. This is the story as she told it to an officer:

'Well, I don't know if you seed him, sir, but down drops poor Dan, to be murdered like all the rest, and says he, "Biddy dear, I can't go no furder one yard to save me life." "O, Dan jewel," sis I, "I'll help you on a bit; tak' a hould of me an' throw away your knapsack." "I'll niver part wid my knapsack," says he, "nor my firelock, while I'm a soger." So I draws him up on the bank and coaxed him to get on me back, for, sis I, "the French will have ye in half an hour, an' me too, the pagans." Well, sir, I went away wid him on me back, knapsack, firelock, and all, as strong as Samson for the fear I was in; an' I carried him half a league after the regiment into the bivwack; an' me back was bruck entirely from that time to this, an' it'll never get straight till I go to the Holy Well in Ireland, and have Father McShane's blessin', and' his hands laid over me!'

Officers could bring their wives with them if they wished. A French prisoner saw a high ranking officer on the march with his family. This is what he wrote:

'The captain rode first on a very fine horse, warding off the sun with a parasol: then came his wife very prettily dressed with a small straw hat, riding on a mule and carrying not a parasol, but a little black and tan dog on her knee, while she led by a cord a she-goat to supply her with milk. Beside madame walked her Irish nurse, carrying in a green silk wrapper a baby, the hope of the family. A grenadier, the captain's servant, came behind and occasionally poked up the long eared steed of his mistress with a staff. Last in the procession came a donkey loaded with much miscellaneous baggage, which included a kettle and a cage of canaries.'

12 Sieges

Opposite you can see a picture of a fortified town. This one still has its medieval walls with their battlements. In front of them you can see the eighteenth-century defences which follow a zigzag line and have a deep ditch. The picture underneath it shows you what it was like in the ditch. The diagram is a cross-section through the defences.

In the plan on page 75 you can see shapes like this ⌐⌐ at intervals. These were called bastions and were where the defenders put their guns. You can see that each bastion had a name. You can imagine that it was not easy to capture a town

Bastions

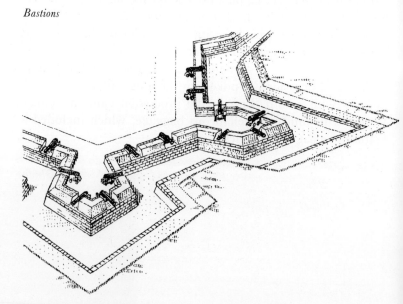

A fortified town

Ditch of a fortification

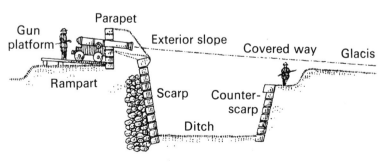

Section through defences

like this. To show you what a siege was like, here is the story of the attack on Badajoz by Wellington's men in 1812.

The siege began on 8 March. The first thing the British did was to mount their heavy guns in batteries. The guns had to have firm platforms, and there had to be earthworks in front of them to protect the gunners from fire from the fortress. Nor was this the only danger. The enemy might make a *sortie* and *spike* the guns. To stop this the besiegers dug a trench in front of the guns and lined it with the troops. This ditch was called a parallel, as it ran roughly parallel with the walls. When all this was finished the guns opened fire. They had two tasks. One was to silence the guns in the fortress, and the other was to smash breaches in the walls.

The digging now began in earnest. So that the attackers could move up to the walls, more or less in safety, someone had to dig trenches for them to walk along. These trenches were called saps, and the men who dug them were sappers. Unfortunately Wellington had few sappers, so he had to use his infantry. The troops hated the work and, since they had no training for it, were not very good at it. The weather did not help, for it rained heavily and filled the trenches with water. Nor was it possible to dig in peace, for the enemy kept up a steady fire and a man in the trenches had to keep his musket handy. Kincaid said it was like being apprenticed to a grave-digger and a gamekeeper at the same time.

But in spite of the difficulties the saps began to draw near the walls and the guns opened up three breaches.

Look at the plan opposite and find the parallel, the batteries, the saps and the breaches.

Meanwhile the French defenders were busy. They made one sortie, but the British drove them off. They laid mines and explosive barrels in the ditch together with all sorts of obstacles —carts, barrows, damaged boats and rope entanglements. They covered the slope of the breaches with spikes and beams studded with nails. At the top of the breaches they put chevaux de frise. These were made from beams a foot square, about three feet above the ground. Set in the beams were dozens of sword
74 blades that stuck out at all angles.

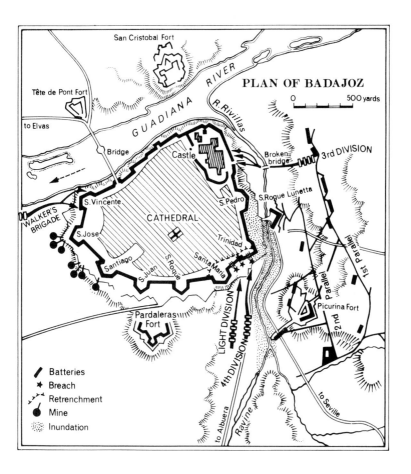

PLAN OF BADAJOZ

0   500 yards

San Cristobal Fort

Tête de Pont Fort

to Elvas

GUADIANA RIVER

R. Rivillas

Bridge

Castle

Broken bridge

3rd DIVISION

WALKER'S BRIGADE

S. Vincente

S. Pedro

S. Roque Lunetta

CATHEDRAL

1st Parallel

S. Jose

Trinidad

Santiago

S. Juan

S. Roque

Santa Maria

2nd Parallel

Picurina Fort

Pardaleras Fort

LIGHT DIVISION

4th DIVISION

to Albuera

Ravine

to Seville

/ Batteries
* Breach
⌁ Retrenchment
● Mine
∷ Inundation

At last, on 6 April Wellington decided it was time to attack.
He ordered the Fourth and Light divisions to storm the
breaches. General Picton came to see Wellington and begged
him for permission to attack the strongest part of the defences—
the castle. Wellington agreed, but the guns had made no breach
in the castle walls, so Picton's men would have to try to carry

75

the place by *escalade*. Finally, at the last minute, Wellington told General Wade to take a brigade of the Fifth Division to storm the bastion of San Vincente in the north-west corner of the town.

The attack began at 10 p.m. The Fourth and Light Divisions both sent forward advance parties of 500 carrying ladders and hay-bags. The hay bags were to drop into the ditch, so that the soldiers could jump down with safety. Others had to run and lie down at the top of the *glacis* to fire at the defenders on the walls. John Kincaid was one of these.

The attackers were soon confused. The Fourth Division found their section of the ditch flooded and, swerving to the left, they ran into the Light Division. Also the French were ready. As soon as the ditch was full of attackers they exploded their mines and opened fire from the walls. John Kincaid said: 'The scene that ensued furnished as respectable a representation of hell itself as fire and sword and human sacrifice could make it: for in one instant every engine of destruction was in full operation.'

Another officer describes what it was like: 'The ramparts crowded with dark figures and glittering arms were on one side, on the other the red columns of the British, deep and broad, were coming on like streams of burning lava; it was the touch of the magician's wand, for a crash of thunder followed and with incredible violence the storming parties were dashed to pieces by the explosion of hundreds of shells and powder barrels.'

The attackers came on again and again and in two hours made forty attacks. But it was all in vain. Very few men even reached the tops of the breaches. In the morning there was one corpse on top of the chevaux de frise and two or three beneath them. No man reached the other side and a quarter of the attackers were killed or wounded.

McGrigor describes Wellington's face as he heard the news: 'I shall never forget it to the last moment of my existence. The jaw had fallen, and the face was of unusual length, while the torchlight gave his countenance a lurid aspect.'

But just when all seemed lost an English bugle sounded in the town. The men of the Fourth and Light Divisions came once more to the breaches, found no one there and stormed into the

Storming a breach

town. What had happened was that both Picton and Wade's second in command Walker had succeeded in their attacks. The defenders had needed so many men at the breaches that the rest of the walls were undermanned.

British troops were now loose in the streets of Badajoz. The defenders were French, but the inhabitants were Spaniards, and our friends and allies. This made no difference. The rules of war said that soldiers who took a town by storm had the right to plunder it, and this they did. The officers wisely left, and for three days the soldiers ran wild. There were the most dreadful atrocities so that these three days are among the blackest in the history of the British army. Finally the looters wore themselves out, and Wellington sent a brigade of Portuguese troops into the town. Also the Provost Marshal set up a gallows. The agony of Badajoz was over.

As we saw on page 65 John Kincaid won a handsome black horse at Badajoz, but another officer did even better. This was Captain Harry Smith. He saved a beautiful Spanish girl, Juana de Leon, and two days later he married her. For the rest of the war Juana cheerfully followed her husband through all dangers and hardships. Later she went with him to South Africa. He was now Lord Harry Smith, and if you look at a map of Natal, you find the compliment that Lord Harry paid to his wife.

13 The Campaign of 1812

In the early part of the war Wellington was on the defensive. The French had too many men in Spain for him to attack them, but he knew he could be a great nuisance to them if he could only hang on to Portugal. The French knew this as well, and in 1810 Marshal Masséna led a large army to capture Lisbon and drive Wellington into the sea. Wellington checked Masséna at the battle of Busaco, but could not stop his advance. Masséna came on and it looked as if the French would swamp the British.

But Wellington had a surprise for them. When they were only thirty miles from Lisbon the French found their way barred by powerful fortifications that they did not dare attack. These were the famous Lines of Torres Vedras. Hundreds of workmen had taken months to build them, but the secret was so well kept that even in the British army most soldiers did not know they were there. To the French the Lines were a complete surprise.

Wellington now watched and waited. He knew the French had no proper supply system and had to live off the country, and he knew Portugal was too poor to feed them for long. Masséna waited through the winter, until his men were dying of starvation at the rate of 500 a week. Then he led the remains of his army back to Spain. The French never again made a serious attack on Portugal.

In 1811, and early in 1812, there was some hard fighting on the frontier. There were four fortresses: Elvas and Almeida in Portugal and Ciudad Rodrigo and Badajoz in Spain. The French did not hold Elvas, but they had the other three. One by one Wellington took them—first Almeida, then Ciudad Rodrigo and, after three attempts, Badajoz. You read about the capture of Badajoz in the last chapter.

If Wellington wanted to go into Spain it was now safe to do so. All he needed was the opportunity, and it was not long coming.

Early in 1812 two things happened which helped Wellington a lot. In the first place, Napoleon decided to invade Russia, and he took many of the best soldiers from Spain. Secondly he ordered Marshal Suchet, the commander of the Army of Aragon, to attack Valencia, which was still held by the Spaniards. You should find Aragon and Valencia on the map on the inside back cover. To help Suchet French troops had to leave the Portuguese frontier and march east.

Wellington decided to attack. You will see from the map where the French armies were. The Army of Portugal was in Spain, because the English had driven it there. This table gives the armies, their commanders and says how strong they were:

French armies in Spain 1812

Army of the North	General Caffarelli	48,000
Army of Aragon	Marshal Suchet	60,000
Army of the South	Marshal Soult	55,000
Army of the Centre	King Joseph	15,000
Army of Portugal	Marshal Marmont	52,000
		———
		230,000
		———

Wellington could put only 66,000 men into the field. How many times did the French outnumber the English? Why was it Wellington thought it was safe to attack?

If you look again at the map you will see there were some Spanish armies. They were weak and inefficient, but even so the French could not ignore them. Also there were guerrillas almost everywhere that there were mountains. If the French evacuated any part of Spain then either a Spanish army or some guerrillas would move in. As a result nearly all the French armies were what we call 'armies of occupation'. They were scattered about in towns and fortresses, or patrolling the roads to keep them open.

The French had a problem. If they joined their armies together, they could drive Wellington back to Portugal—but then they would lose large parts of Spain to the Spanish forces.

If they held on to the land they had conquered, then Wellington had the chance to defeat their armies one by one. As Napoleon had ordered them to hold on to as much of Spain as possible, they took this risk. In fact there was just one army they could use against Wellington without giving up any territory, and that was the army of Portugal under Marmont. Marmont's men had no occupation duties. Why not?

There was just a chance that Soult might send help to Marmont as he did have a few men to spare. To stop this Wellington gave General Hill 18,000 men, and sent him to

Marshall Marmont

Estremadura to keep an eye on Soult. With the rest of his army Wellington prepared to go into Leon to attack Marmont.

The Campaign of Salamanca

Wellington advanced into Leon in June. He had with him 48,000 infantry, 3,500 cavalry and 54 guns. He arrived at Salamanca and caught Marmont unawares. The army of Portugal was scattered round the countryside and there was a large detachment under Bonnet far away in the Asturias. Wellington had a chance to do much damage to Marmont's army before it gathered together, but he was hoping to fight a defensive battle which he knew he would probably win. So he laid siege to some forts the French had built in Salamanca, and placed the rest of his army in an excellent position outside the town. He hoped Marmont would attack in order to save the forts in Salamanca. This nearly happened. Gathering the forces near at hand—about 30,000 of them—Marmont hurried to Salamanca where he found a force of 40,000 waiting for him. 81

He pushed his own army well up to them and prepared to attack. He was saved from himself by one of his most able generals, General Foy, who told him that an attack would be suicide. But the French were now in a dreadful position. Wellington was right on top of them and had he ordered an attack he would probably have destroyed Marmont's army easily. But once again Wellington hesitated and missed his opportunity. Marmont slipped away and. went north of the Duero where he waited for Bonnet to come back from the Asturias.

Wellington followed, but it was not long before Bonnet returned and Marmont felt he could go over to the attack. He knew that Wellington had already thrown away two opportunities and felt he was quite safe to move against him. On 16 July he crossed the river Duero and marched south, trying to swing round behind the English army and cut off its communications with Portugal. Wellington pulled back towards Salamanca to prevent this. On 20 July the two armies met but

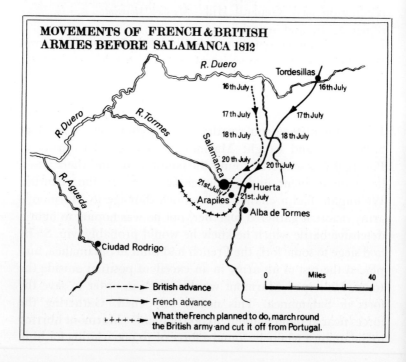

MOVEMENTS OF FRENCH & BRITISH
ARMIES BEFORE SALAMANCA 1812

R. Duero

Tordesillas

16th July

16th July

17th July

17th July

18th July

18th July

R. Tormes

Salamanca

20th July

20th July

R. Duero

21st July

Huerta

21st July

Arapiles

R. Agueda

Alba de Tormes

Ciudad Rodrigo

0   Miles   40

------▶ British advance

——▶ French advance

++++▶ What the French planned to do, march round
the British army and cut it off from Portugal.

Wellington refused battle and moved to the West. That meant that Marmont, too, was able to swing to the west. Also his army that day marched fifteen miles. Wellington's men had only managed twelve.

Time was running out for the British. Marmont's plans were succeeding. He was already gaining on his enemies. Soon Wellington would have to fight a battle or lose Salamanca. So far he had been quite unwilling to risk an attack on the French.

On 21 July both armies crossed the Tormes, the British near Salamanca, and the French at the fords of Huerta. That night there was a thunderstorm. Lieutenant Tomkinson stood in the darkness, and each time the lightning flashed he saw it glint on the muskets of the columns of infantry as they moved into position for a most uncomfortable night. The horses of the Dragoon Guards stampeded, ran away over the men of the regiment as they lay on the ground, and injured eighteen of them. A Colonel Dalbiac found himself in the path of the horses and his wife was beside him. He just had time to drag her under a gun carriage, and they both lay there while the hooves pounded within a few inches of their heads.

Private Wheeler was miserable. He was sheltering as best he could under an oak tree and the only comfort he had was his pipe. Even that refused to light, so he ran through the rain to a friend. When he came back his oak tree had been struck by lightning and split from top to bottom. 'That,' he said to himself, 'was a lucky pipe of tobacco.'

The battle of Salamanca

On the morning of 22 July both armies were inside the great bend of the river Tormes. The British were in *undulating* country north of the village of Arapiles. Just to the east of this village are the twin hills that give the village its name—the North Arapile and the South Arapile. You can see them on the map and there is a picture of one of them on page 85.

Marmont's army was the other side of the little river Pelagarcia. His troops had reached as far as Calvarisa de Ariba. Looking west towards the British, Marmont could see little for the hills shielded Wellington's men. There was just one division

The Battle of Salamanca

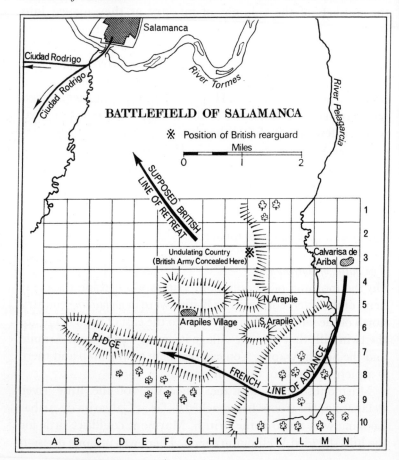

Salamanca

Ciudad Rodrigo

Ciudad Rodrigo

River Tormes

River Pelagarcia

BATTLEFIELD OF SALAMANCA

✳ Position of British rearguard

Miles

0   1   2

SUPPOSED BRITISH LINE OF RETREAT

Undulating Country
(British Army Concealed Here)

Calvarisa de Ariba

N. Arapile

Arapiles Village

S. Arapile

RIDGE

FRENCH LINE OF ADVANCE

1
2
3
4
5
6
7
8
9
10

A   B   C   D   E   F   G   H   I   J   K   L   M   N

The South Arapile

near at hand, obviously the rearguard, while far away in the
distance there was a thin column of troops moving away
towards Ciudad Rodrigo. This was the English baggage train.
What lay between Marmont could only guess, but to him it was
obvious. The English army was in full retreat, and if he hurried
he could cut off the rearguard and destroy it. He ordered
Bonnet with his division to occupy the South Arapile. Foy and
Ferrey were to remain at Calvarisa to guard the rear. The rest
of the army was to march through the woods behind Bonnet and
push forward along the ridge which runs south of the village of

the British army in the flank. Marmont was so sure of success
that he sent a message to Salamanca and ordered his former
landlord to prepare his dinner.

General Thomières pushed boldly along the ridge with his
division. General Maucune halted his men opposite the village
of Arapiles and his artillery opened fire. Generals Brennier and
Clausel were coming hot-foot through the woods behind. It
seemed to Marmont that his army would soon sweep round the
flank of the British and cut off their rearguard. Indeed this must
have happened, but for one thing. Wellington's army was not in
retreat; it was waiting behind the hills. General Foy wrote
later on: 'The wily Wellington was ready to give battle—the
greater part of his host was collected, but behind the line of

heights: he was showing nothing on the crest: he was waiting for our movement.'

Marmont had made a dreadful mistake. From Thomières' division away on his left, to Foy's back in Calvarisa de Ariba, there was a distance of six miles. His divisions were strung out and separated, while the English army was concentrated into a small area. If Wellington would only attack, he might defeat the French divisions one by one. He had already thrown away two good chances: now Marmont had given him a third. But would he attack? One of his staff describes what happened:

'Lord Wellington had given his glass to an aide-de-camp, while he himself sat down to eat a few mouthfuls of cold beef. Presently the officer reported that the enemy were still extending to their left. "The devil they are! Give me the glass quickly," said his lordship—and then after a long inspection, "This will do at last, I think—ride off."'

First of all Wellington galloped over to the Third Division which was commanded by his brother-in-law, Edward Pakenham. He ordered him to attack the west end of the ridge and carry everything before him. Wellington then came back to the rest of the army. James Leith with the fifth division was to attack Maucune. Protecting his right flank he had Bradford's Portuguese brigade, and behind him he had John Hope's Seventh Division. Next, Lowry Cole with the Fourth Division was to attack Clausel. He had Pack's Portuguese brigade on his left, and the Sixth Division under Henry Clinton was behind him, in support.

The first blow came from the Third Division. Pakenham's men marched to the western edge of the ridge and *deployed* into line without even bothering to halt. Further along, Thomières' men still thought that the British army was in retreat. They advanced without even bothering to send forward a screen of tirailleurs. The first shock came when a small group of Portuguese cavalry smashed into their leading troops and sent them flying. Almost at once Pakenham's leading brigade appeared, strung across the front of the French column in their long thin line. Every man in the British line could fire his musket and volley after volley thundered out. As usual, only a few of the

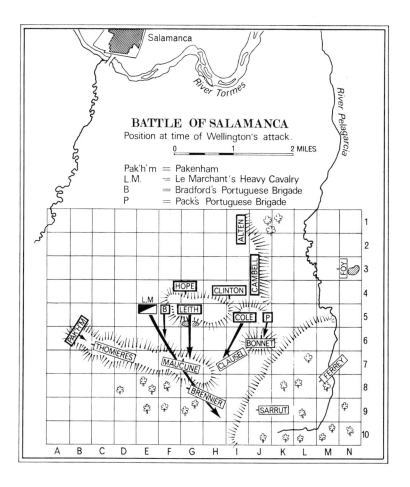

BATTLE OF SALAMANCA

Position at time of Wellington's attack.

0   1   2 MILES

Pak'h'm = Pakenham
L.M.   = Le Marchant's Heavy Cavalry
B   = Bradford's Portuguese Brigade
P   = Pack's Portuguese Brigade

leading French troops could reply and it was not long before Thomières's men were streaming back the way they had come, leaving their general dead on the field.

As soon as Leith heard the roll of Pakenham's volleys, he sent his Fifth Division against Maucune. Along with Bradford's Portuguese he had 8,300 men, and Maucune had only 5,000. Moreover Maucune had placed his men in squares. This would have been a good formation to meet cavalry, but against infantry it was hopeless. Only the men facing the English could fire, but every man in the English line could reply. Leith's men

87

shot Maucune's squares to pieces and just as the French were wavering, they saw a terrible sight. Over the brow of the hill a thousand English cavalry came at the gallop. This was the heavy brigade under General Le Marchant. All discipline gone, Maucune's men fled in terror. Le Marchant's men swept over them and the Fifth Division had only to round up prisoners. Nor did Le Marchant stop there. Brennier's Division had just arrived and the Heavy Brigade went at it full tilt. The French opened fire at a range of ten yards; a quarter of the English cavalry fell—but the rest charged on. Steady infantry could always beat off cavalry, but Brennier's men had just come a mile at a steady run—they were confused and out of breath. The cavalry scared them completely and they joined Maucune's men, running away in wild confusion. Some of them were so frantic they even fled to the English infantry! An officer in the 88th regiment said: 'Hundreds of men, frightfully disfigured, black with dust, worn out with fatigue and covered with sabre cuts and blood, threw themselves among us for safety.'

Le Marchant's charge delighted Wellington. 'By God,' he said, 'I never saw anything so beautiful in my life.' But General Le Marchant was shot dead.

So far three French divisions had been routed, but elsewhere things were not going so well for the allies.

Lowry Cole led his Fourth Division to attack Clausel, but he had less men than Clausel. Also on his flank was the Greater Arapile, held by General Bonnet with the largest division in the French Army—over 6,000 strong. To distract Bonnet Wellington ordered Pack to attack him with his Portuguese Brigade, which had only 2,600 men. Of course this was hopeless. Pack's Portuguese did not even reach the top of the hill before they were driven back in confusion. Meanwhile Clausel had fought off Cole, and Bonnet's men fell on his flank. The Fourth Division broke and fled. This was the crisis of the battle.

Unfortunately for the French, Marmont had been wounded earlier on and Clausel was now in command. What was he to do? If he stopped his attack he might take advantage of the confusion to lead much of the army of Portugal to safety. But there was a gap in the British line and he saw that if he poured the men of his own and Bonnet's divisions through it, he could snatch victory out of defeat. Furthermore General Sarrut was now at last leading his Division into action. Clausel ordered an attack.

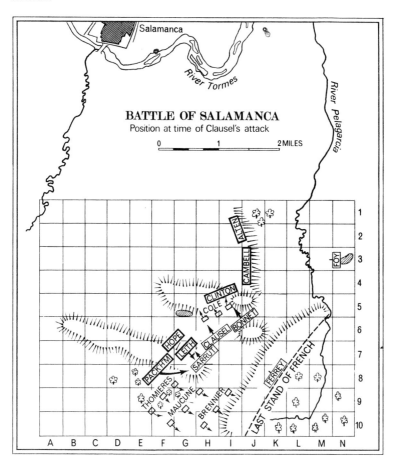

BATTLE OF SALAMANCA
Position at time of Clausel's attack

0   1   2 MILES

But Wellington was ready. Henry Clinton was close at hand with the Sixth Division and Wellington ordered him forward. The columns of Bonnet's division ran into the line of Clinton's division, with the usual result. As they fled, Clausel's men turned and ran with them. Meanwhile Pakenham's and Leith's Divisions had routed Sarrut's men, so that the French now had only two divisions left. One was Foy's, but that was too far away. The other was Ferrey's, and Clausel turned to him in despair. At all costs, he said, Ferrey must hold off the British. The rest of the army of Portugal was running away and unless they had time to escape, many thousands of them would be lost. Ferrey did his best. Probably his men were the real heroes of the day. They drew up in line, which was most unusual for the French, and as the Sixth Division surged forward, they had a nasty shock. They met a French Division in which every man could use his musket. This was how it looked from the English side:

'The glare of light caused by the artillery, the continued fire of the musketry, and by the dry grass which had caught fire, gave the face of the hill a terrific grandeur; it was one sheet of flame and Clinton's men seemed to be attacking a burning mountain whose crater was defended by a barrier of shining steel.'

This was how the French saw things:

'Formed right up against the trees we saw the enemy marching up against us in two lines, the first of which was composed of Portuguese. Our position was critical, but we waited for the shock. The two lines moved up towards us: their order was so regular that in the Portuguese regiment in front of us we could see the officers keeping the men in accurate line by blows with the flat of their swords or their canes. We fired first, the moment that they got within range, and our volleys were so heavy and continuous that the whole melted away. The second line was coming up behind—this was English. We should have tried to receive it in the same way, when suddenly the left of our line fell back in complete disorder. The 70th Ligne had found itself turned by cavalry: it broke.'

Ferrey's men had held long enough to allow most of the fugitives to escape, but now they too, joined the route. One of the officers said: 'A shapeless mass of soldiery was rolling down the road like a torrent—infantry, cavalry, artillery, waggons, carts, baggage mules, the reserve park of the artillery drawn by oxen were all mixed up. The men, shouting, swearing, running, were all out of order, each looking after himself alone—a complete stampede.'

What was Wellington to do now? He had used neither his

Seventh Division nor his First Division. There was also a lot of cavalry in hand. But Clinton's battered and weary Sixth Division was the only one he ordered to pursue the French. Not surprisingly they caught very few. Nor was this the only mistake. The French army was fleeing towards the river Tormes, at a place where they could only cross it by one bridge, which was in the little town of Alba de Tormes. Here there was supposed to be a force of Spaniards, who could easily have kept the defeated army from crossing. For no good reason at all the Spaniards had marched away the day before, and the French poured over the bridge with no one to stop them.

Salamanca was a great victory. Wellington's army lost 5,000 men, while the French lost well over 14,000. But the French army of Portugal had escaped—and it was later to have its revenge.

Madrid and Burgos

The army of Portugal fled north, over the river Duero, and the only army that lay between Wellington and Madrid was the tiny Army of the Centre under King Joseph. Joseph fled with his men to join Marshal Suchet in Valencia.

Wellington's army entered Madrid on 12 August. Private Wheeler describes what it was like to march through the streets:

'In one place would be a brawny Spaniard with a pigskin of wine, filling vessels for us to drink, then another with a basket full of bread distributing it around, then a pretty, palefaced, black-eyed maid would modestly offer a nosegay or a sprig of olive, whilst others of the sex more bold would dash into our ranks, take off our caps and place a sprig of laurel, then without ceremony seize our arm and sing some martial air.

'But amidst all this pleasure and happiness we were obliged to submit to a custom so un-English that I cannot but feel disgust. It was to be kissed by the men. What made it still worse, their breath was so highly seasoned with garlick, then their huge mustaches well stiffened with sweat, dust and snuff, it was like having a hair broom pushed into one's face that had been daubed in a dirty gutter.'

After all their hard marching and fighting, the soldiers enjoyed themselves in Madrid. They were free to go everywhere, even to the royal gardens where they ate the fruit and caught and fried the goldfish—a strange meal that gave them stomach-ache.

But Wellington had more to worry about than indigestion. There was bad news coming in. Far away in the south Marshal Soult, after a lot of grumbling, agreed to obey King Joseph and give up Andalusia. He was marching to join Joseph. If you look at the table on page 80 you will see that the two armies together would be very powerful. Nor was this all. In the north the Army of Portugal had got over its defeat and was once again being a nuisance.

What would you have done in Wellington's position? Obviously if Soult was in Valencia, there was no point in keeping Hill in Estremadura, so Wellington ordered him to come to Madrid. His own army he divided into two. Three divisions stayed in Madrid to wait for Hill while he took the other four to finish the work he had begun at Salamanca. He hoped he could destroy the Army of Portugal before Soult's army came too close.

Marshall Soult

Almost at once things began to go wrong. Wellington advanced very carefully. On 12 September he reached Valladolid, and a few days later he was at Burgos. You should find these places on the map at the end of the book. But Wellington had advanced so slowly that the Army of Portugal had no trouble in escaping. Moreover, the British did not go beyond Burgos. Wellington decided that he must take the castle there. Unfortunately his siege guns were back in Madrid. He had left them behind so that his Army could move quickly. The attacks on Burgos failed. Wellington managed to find three small cannon, but there were many more against him in the castle. He tried digging mines under the walls; he tried assaulting the castle without making a breach. It was all in vain, and valuable days and weeks slipped by. Wellington wasted a whole month at Burgos, and meanwhile the French had not been idle. In the first place they had built up the Army of Portugal until it was 50,000 strong. Wellington had only 35,000 with him, of whom 11,000 were Spaniards. Back in Madrid Hill had 30,000 men, but Soult and Joseph were marching from Valencia with 60,000.

All the British could do was to retreat. You can find out from the map which way they went. Hill joined Wellington at Salamanca on 10 November, and on the 15th the British once again faced the French on the old battlefield. The horses kicked up the skulls of men who had died in the first battle of Salamanca and it looked as if there would be a second battle on the same spot. But the French had learnt their lesson. Soult had charge of their army. He refused to attack Wellington, but instead moved west to cut the English off from Portugal. Unlike Marmont, Soult did not let his divisions scatter. He kept them well in hand and Wellington did not dare attack either. Instead he ordered his army to retreat to Ciudad Rodrigo.

The next three days were dreadful. In the first place it hardly stopped raining, and secondly the commissary sent the mules carrying the food the wrong way. The army had no proper supplies. This stupidity caused as much hardship and misery as a battle would have done.

This is how a soldier called Ned Costello describes the march:

'The rain fell in torrents, and from the heaviness of the roads, which were in many places a foot deep in mud, most of our men lost their shoes and were obliged to march barefooted.

'On our halt, the first thing I did was to take off my jacket and shirt, and after wringing about half a gallon of water out of them, I replaced them upon my back to dry as they might. Most of our men employed themselves in cutting down branches of trees to keep themselves out of the mud; but it was some hours before we could obtain that greatest of luxuries, a good fire. Still we had not a morsel to eat and our men suffered from all the pangs of cold and hunger.'

This is what another soldier says:

'A savage sort of desperation had taken possession of our minds, and those who lived on the most friendly terms in happier times, now quarrelled with each other, using the most frightful *imprecations* at the slightest offence. The streams were swelled into rivers which we had to wade and many fell out, including even officers. It was piteous to see some of the men who had dragged their limbs after them with determined spirit, fall down at last among the mud, unable to proceed further. Towards night the rain had somewhat abated, but the cold was excessive and numbers who had resisted the effect of hunger and fatigue with a hardy spirit were now obliged to give way, and sank to the ground praying for death to deliver them from their misery. Some prayed not in vain, for next morning I stumbled over several who had died in the night.'

Fortunately there were some store bullocks with the army, so the men had a little beef. The Third Division was lucky. A herd of pigs stampeded and ran into their ranks. The men shot the pigs and cut them to pieces with their bayonets. The only other thing they had to eat was acorns.

What were the French doing while the British struggled through the mud and rain? Happily for Wellington their supplies had broken down as well. You will remember that they expected to live off the country and all this part of Spain had to offer was a few half wild pigs and acorns. They had to break up their huge army and only Soult with the Army of the South went

94

after Wellington. The French too, suffered. They were wet through as well, and they did not like acorns either.

On 19 November the worst was over. Soult retreated, Wellington's men reached Ciudad Rodrigo, and, even more important, the supply train had found its way back to the army. One soldier wrote: 'We had not long been halted when the well-known summons of "turn-out for biscuit" rang in our ears. The strongest went to it and received two days' rations for each man. It was customary to make an orderly division, but that night each eagerly seized what he could get and endeavoured to allay the dreadful gnawing which had tormented us during four days of unexampled cold and fatigue.'

The retreat from Burgos and Madrid cost Wellington 5,000 men—as many as he had lost at the Battle of Salamanca.

Results of the Campaign of 1812

Wellington's men must have been in despair. They had defeated the French in a great battle and had entered Madrid in triumph. They had marched hundreds of miles and had suffered terrible hardships. Now here they were, back on the frontier of Portugal, exactly where they had started at the beginning of the campaign.

But things were not as bad as they seemed. You will remember that the French could only drive Wellington back by joining their armies together. But if they did that, then they would have to give up large parts of Spain. This was just what had happened. Soult joined the Army of the Centre and the Army of Portugal, but he had to leave Andalusia to the Spaniards. At the beginning of 1812 the French still hoped they would conquer the whole of Spain; at the end of 1812 they did not have any troops south of the Tagus, and they had given up all hope of winning the war in the Peninsula.

Through the winter Wellington's men slowly got better. Sir James McGrigor and his doctors were busy, and by the spring of 1813 most of the men were fit. Wellington again attacked. His army stormed through northern Spain, and smashed King Joseph's army at the Battle of Vittoria. By the end of 1813 the British had crossed the Pyrenees, and in 1814 Wellington was

95

winning victories in the south of France until news came that Napoleon had surrendered.

Of course the really big victories against the French took place in Russia and Germany, and you should read about these in your other history books. But in helping to overthrow Napoleon, Wellington's army had done far more, in proportion to its size, than any other army in Europe.

14 *Epilogue—Waterloo*

When Napoleon surrendered in 1814 the allies banished him to
Elba and then sent their envoys to Vienna to make a peace
treaty. Wellington's army split up. Some units came home, but
many crossed the Atlantic to fight against France's ally, the
United States. Then, in 1815 Napoleon escaped from Elba and
the allies had to prepare again for war.

In Belgium a mixed force of Dutch, Belgian and British
troops gathered together. The Duke of Wellington was ordered
to command them. There was also a Prussian army in Belgium,
under Blücher.

Blücher

Most of Napoleon's old soldiers had joined him, but he knew he was in danger. Powerful armies surrounded France, and if they attacked together he knew they would defeat him. His only hope was to smash them one by one.

His first victims were to be the British and Prussians who were in Belgium. The Prussians under Blücher met the French at Ligny on 16 June. Napoleon beat them and they fled. But their army was not destroyed and luckily they did not go east towards home, but north to Wavre. This meant they could still keep in touch with the British, who were commanded by Wellington.

Having, as he thought, finished Blücher, Napoleon went on to deal with Wellington. Parts of both armies clashed at Quatre Bras on 16 June and the British fell back to Waterloo. Here Wellington gathered all his army. Napoleon came up, and on 18 June both sides were ready for battle.

Wellington's old enemy, Soult, was with Napoleon and he warned him that the battle would be difficult. This was the first time Napoleon had faced the British and he scorned Soult's warning. He said, 'Because you have been defeated by Wellington, you think him a great general! I tell you that Wellington is a bad general, that the English are bad troops and that this will be a picnic!'

Wellington was not so happy. Someone asked him if he thought he was going to win. The Duke pointed to a red coated soldier. 'It all depends,' he said, 'on that article there.' But he knew that 'that article' was in short supply. Too many of the veterans of the Peninsular War were across the Atlantic, fighting the Americans. The British that faced the French were mostly raw soldiers who had never been in battle. Many of the Belgian troops ran away as soon as they could, plundering the British baggage waggons as they went.

Their commander, the young Prince of Orange, was ashamed of his men, but putting on a bold face he said to a Spanish friend, General Alava, 'Well, what do you think your Spaniards would have done?' 'Your Highness,' said Alava, 'I do not think they would have run away, as your Belgians did, before the FIRST shot was fired.'

The night before the battle the rain fell in torrents. William Wheeler said: 'The ground was too wet to lie down; we sat on our knapsacks until daylight, without fires; there was no shelter against the weather; the water ran in streams from the cuffs of our jackets; in short we were as wet as if we had been plunged over our heads in a river.' But the old Peninsular veterans remembered the rain and thunder of the night before Salamanca. To them the storm was a good omen.

Because he was so uncertain of his army, Wellington did not dare attack. Instead he got ready for a defensive battle—the kind he had fought in the early days in Spain and Portugal. He put most of his army behind the long ridge that runs east and west, to the south of Waterloo. He also sent forward a screen of light infantry and put reliable troops in the big country house of Hougoumont, and the farms of La Haye Sainte, La Haye and Papelotte.

Things went wrong on both sides. Blücher promised to be at Waterloo early in the day. The first Prussians did not arrive until

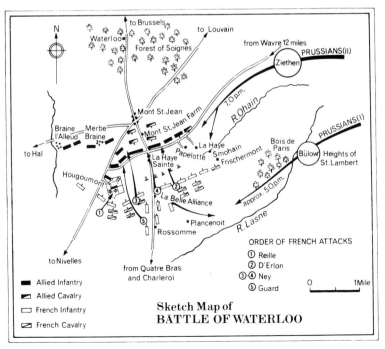

Sketch Map of
BATTLE OF WATERLOO

4 p.m. So many Belgians fled at the first French attack that the allied line nearly broke. The English cavalry lived up to their tradition of 'galloping at everything'. True, they saved the day in a famous charge that smashed D'Erlon's infantry just as they were about to break our line; but they then chased the fugitives much too far—in fact right up to the main French Army. They then tried to escape. Their tired horses could barely move in the deep mud and the French cavalry cut them to pieces.

The French made even worse mistakes. Napoleon was no longer the dashing young general. He was a fat little middle-aged man. Also he had piles, so that it was agony for him to sit on a horse. At one point in the battle, he waddled off, his legs wide apart, so that he could dress his sores.

The French attack should have begun at 9 a.m. This would have left them plenty of time to defeat Wellington before

Grenadier of the Imperial Guard

Cavalry of the Imperial Guard

Blücher arrived. In fact they did not attack until 11.30 a.m. The splendid troops of the Imperial Guard were used up in several unimportant attacks. If Napoleon had flung them all in at just the right moment, he might well have won the battle. But probably the worst mistake was to send some 9,000 cavalry into the attack without any proper support from infantry or artillery. Wellington's infantry formed squares and shot the French cavalry to pieces as they galloped helplessly round them.

The French attacked again and again. They did make some progress and captured La Haye Sainte. But they could go no further. More and more men fell on both sides and John Kincaid said: 'I had never yet heard of a battle in which everybody was killed, but this seemed likely as an exception as all were going by turns.'

At last the Prussians began to arrive. At first the French drove back their leading troops quite easily, but when the main force came up the French turned and fled. John Kincaid describes the end. The smoke had been so thick that he had seen next to nothing for hours. He now went forward through the smoke, and this is what he saw:

'It was a fine summer's evening, just before sunset. The French were flying in one confused mass. British lines were seen in close pursuit, and in admirable order, as far as the eye could reach to the right, while the plain to the left was filled with Prussians. Artillery, baggage and everything belonging to them fell into our hands. After pursuing them until dark, we halted about two miles beyond the field of battle, leaving the Prussians to follow up the victory.'

Things To Do

1 Find out what you can about the Battle of Vimiero and the Convention of Cintra 1808.

2 Find out what you can about Sir John Moore's expedition to Spain 1808–09.

3 Draw a sketch map of Spain showing the main towns, provinces, rivers and mountains.

4 Imagine you are an officer in Wellington's army. Write a letter home saying what you think of Spain and the Spaniards.

5 Imagine you are a recruiting serjeant. Describe how you persuade men to join the army.

6 Imagine you have just joined the army. Write a letter to a friend telling him about your uniform and equipment.

7 Imagine you are an English infantryman. Describe how your division beat off an attack by some French columns.

8 Describe the work of a commissary and explain how important it was for the army.

9 Describe the work done by army doctors after a battle.

10 You have been wounded in battle. Write a letter home saying what happened.

11 Describe an ordinary day in the life of one of Wellington's men. Do not include any fighting.

12 You have been on picket duty. Write an account of your experiences.

13   You are a cavalry officer. Describe what happened when you were one of an advance guard.

14   Imagine you were a French soldier defending one of the breaches at Badajoz in 1812. Say what happened.

15   Read the book in this series called 'Nelson's Navy'. Organise a class debate on the proposal: 'This class thinks that Nelson's sailors led a harder life than Wellington's soldiers.'

16   Imagine you are Wellington. It is May 1812. Write a letter home describing the situation in the Peninsula and explaining why you have decided to invade Spain.

17   Imagine you are each of the following in turn and describe the part you played in the Battle of Salamanca: *(a)* A cavalry soldier in the Heavy Brigade; *(b)* General Clausel; *(c)* A soldier in the British Sixth Division.

18   You are an infantry soldier who has just reached Ciudad Rodrigo after the retreat from Burgos. Describe what happened during the retreat.

19   Find out what you can about Wellington's life both before and after the period covered by this book.

20   Visit your local museum. See if you can find any uniforms, weapons or other relics of Wellington's times.

Further Reading

There are many good books written by soldiers of Wellington's time. Here are some you would enjoy.

The Wheatley Diary, edited by Christopher Hibbert. Longmans, 1964.
EDWARD COSTELLO, *Adventures of a Soldier,* edited by Anthony Brett James. Longmans, 1966.
Thomas Morris, edited by John Selby. Longmans, 1967.
The Letters of Private Wheeler, edited by Captain B. H. Liddell Hart. Michael Joseph, 1951.
The Recollections of Rifleman Harris, edited by Henry Curling. Peter Davies, 1929.
JOHN KINCAID, *Adventures in the Rifle Brigade,* edited by Sir John Fortescue. Peter Davies, 1929.

Glossary

address, bearing, manner

asunder, apart

banditti, bandits

beau, handsome, well-dressed man

bespeak, to ask for

biscuit, ship's biscuit; these were dry, hard and unsweetened; often used instead of bread, because they kept longer.

boat cloak, an officer's cloak, so called because it was a kind of cloak first used in the navy.

bolero, lively Spanish dance, for one or several couples, invented about 1780

bounty money, money paid to a man when he volunteered to be a soldier

brunette, girl or woman with very dark hair and eyes.

caçadores, Portuguese Light Infantry: the word means 'hunters'

canteen, water bottle

carbine, short musket

cartouche box, box in which a soldier carried his ammunition.

commission, document giving a man authority as an officer.

coercive measures, actions taken to compel people to do something they do not want to do.

court martial, military court that tried the more important offences

delirious, wandering in the mind.

deploy, to spread troops out in a line.

depôt, headquarters of a regiment where its recruits came for training and where it kept its stores.

do, to get by cheating

dollar, Spanish coin worth about five shillings

dragoon, cavalryman

ensign, the lowest rank of officer

entrenching tool, tool used for digging trenches.

escalade, scaling a fortress with ladders.

fandango, lively Spanish dance, for one couple; perhaps came from South America

farrier, man who looks after horses in a cavalry regiment

fillip, bit of encouragement

flank, the extreme left or right of a body of troops.

glacis, gently sloping mound in front of fortifications, made to protect the walls against gun fire: see diagram on page

grape shot, large number of small iron balls shot from a cannon: see chapter 8

guerrilla, man carrying on irregular warfare.

haversack, stout canvas bag strapped to the back

Iberian Peninsula, the land occupied by Spain and Portugal

imprecation, curse

junta, council

knapsack, see haversack

limber, front part of a gun carriage, made up of two wheels, the pole for the horses, and one or two ammunition boxes; it was unhooked from the rest of the carriage when the gun was to fire.

manoeuvre, to move about in an orderly way on the battle field.

matador, bull fighter

match, cord soaked in a solution of saltpetre and dried, then wrapped round a stick and used to fire a gun. It burnt very slowly, like the fuse of a firework.

militia, soldiers enlisted to defend the area in which they live: militia never served far from home

muleteer, man who looks after a mule train

murphy, slang name for a potato

muleteer, man who looks after a mule train

nauseous, unpleasant

orderly, hospital attendant

pannier, basket

parapet, the top of a wall

pelisse, kind of cloak

poltroon, worthless person

precipitate, hasty

ravine, deep, narrow valley, or a gorge

regulars, the regular army

rifle, gun with corkscrew-like grooves cut in the barrel to make the bullet spin

sabre, cavalry sword

scabbard, sheath for a sword

sortie, attack made by the garrison of a fortress against the troops besieging it

spike, to drive a nail in the vent of a gun to put it out of action

talisman, magic charm

tirailleur, French sharp shooter

undulating, uneven

vidette, sentry (probably comes from 'vedere' which is Italian for 'to see'): videttes were the eyes of the army.

volley, large number of muskets fired at the same time

wood party, group of men sent to collect wood for fires